NAVAL
EXPEDITIONS

NAVAL EXPEDITIONS
The French Return to Indochina, 1945–1946

Charles W. Koburger, Jr.

Foreword by
Admiral Yves Leenhardt, French Navy (Ret.)

Westport, Connecticut
London

Library of Congress Cataloging-in-Publication Data

Koburger, Charles W.
  Naval expeditions : the French return to Indochina, 1945–1946 /
Charles W. Koburger, Jr. ; foreword by Admiral Yves Leenhardt.
    p.   cm.
  Includes bibliographical references and index.
  ISBN 0–275–95982–1 (alk. paper)
  1. Indochina—History—1945–   2. France—History, Naval—20th
century.   I. Title.
DS550.K59   1997
959—dc21   97–2247

British Library Cataloguing in Publication Data is available.

Copyright © 1997 by Charles W. Koburger, Jr.

All rights reserved. No portion of this book may be
reproduced, by any process or technique, without the
express written consent of the publisher.

Library of Congress Catalog Card Number: 97–2247
ISBN: 0–275–95982–1

First published in 1997

Praeger Publishers, 88 Post Road West, Westport, CT 06881
An imprint of Greenwood Publishing Group, Inc.

Printed in the United States of America

The paper used in this book complies with the
Permanent Paper Standard issued by the National
Information Standards Organization (Z39.48–1984).

10 9 8 7 6 5 4 3 2 1

For the U.S. Marine Corps
A thinking Marine is the most dangerous kind

CONTENTS

Maps	ix
Foreword *by Admiral Yves Leenhardt, French Navy (ret.)*	xi
Preface	xiii
Acknowledgments	xv
Introduction	1
1. Prologue: World War II	11
2. The Expedition Is Formed	21
3. The Problem	31
4. Cochin-China (Saigon)	41
5. The Mekong Delta and South Annam	53
6. Tonkin	69
7. Bentré	81
8. The Landing	95
9. Epilogue	105

Conclusion	115
Appendixes	125
Selected Bibliography	141
Index	145

A photographic essay follows page 52.

MAPS

I–1.	Indochina	5
4–1.	Mekong Delta	42
6–1.	Tonkin	71
7–1.	Haiphong and Approaches	86

FOREWORD

It is for me a pleasure and an honor to introduce this new work by Captain Koburger. The author understands the contemporary French Navy. His preceding works testify to that. He has always drawn on the best references for his history, showing how the French Navy overcame the morale and material problems that it faced during and after World War II. Nothing could be better than that he present to the American public the story of the French return to the Far East.

It is the military operations involved in this return—as well as the politico-military environment in which they took place—that Captain Koburger describes for us. Intended initially to reestablish France in what it considered its rights, these difficult immediate postwar operations eventually worked themselves out as only the first episode in the long Far Eastern confrontation between East and West. When that became apparent, the United States did not spare its support until finally they themselves took over the fight twenty years later.

The author has well grasped the facts of those initial two tumultuous years, the ideas of those who commanded the operations, and the conduct of those who had to execute them. He knows our country, our national mentality, and the difficult situations that our generation overcame. I recommend this book, as I do his others about us.

ADMIRAL YVES LEENHARDT
Former Chief of Naval Staff
President, Académie de Marine, Paris

PREFACE

My *The French Navy in Indochina: Riverine and Coastal Forces, 1945–54* (New York: Praeger, 1991) preceded this book by six years. Covering a ten-year period, the earlier work paints with a broader and therefore shallower brush. This new book covers only the first two years of the previous work. Because it is narrower in scope, this book can—and does—reach deeper into the story. Not all of the research material was even to be had, earlier.

The story of the expedition France sent to recover Indochina over half a century ago (1945–1946) deserves to be told in more detail, to honor brave men if nothing else. But the story of that expedition is full of experiences and politico-military lessons—and warnings—of potentially great value to those who would project power from the sea east of Suez, today. The operational art has not changed much—if any—in those fifty years.

As it turned out, this book acknowledgedly ended up heavily weighted toward the naval aspects of what was intended to be a French joint expedition. This was not intentional. It just turned out that way during the course of the research. The key elements of the story mesh closely with Admiral Owens' concept of such forces, outlined at the beginning of the introduction. Expeditionary warfare is mutatis mutandis bound to be like this.

This book is intended to be a professional military view of what transpired out there in Indochina. It is not—repeat not—a political treatise. Much misinformation about this period in Indochina masquerades as history. It is to be hoped that an accurate, balanced representation of the facts has here been presented. Some of these facts may be a surprise to you. The French have their story, too.

Geographic names and their spellings when writing about the Far East have as usual troubled me. In the end, those employed in this book are again those in use by the participants at the time. They are admittedly a mixture of French, Annamese, and sometimes even English. Any attempt to standardize these names would only cut the reader off from the available basic sources.

ACKNOWLEDGMENTS

French Rear Admiral Jean Kessler (then active chief of the Service Historique de la Marine), Rear Admirals Henri Labrousse and Bernard Estival (both retired), Captain Jean Quéguiner (retired), and noted French historian Philippe Masson all helped, each in his own way. I am proud to acknowledge that help.

Special thanks are due to Bob and JoEllen Godfrey, good neighbors, for their administrative support during the time I researched and wrote this book. They helped materially, and I thank them again.

So also to Ms. Janet Deitz, queen bee of the Astoria and keeper of the copy machine. How ever did anyone write before copy machines?

Last but not least, thanks are due Jason Azze, my production editor. He is the best Praeger has ever provided me.

In spite of all, it is the author alone who is responsible for this book and for any errors of omission or commission it may contain. Sometimes I did not take even good advice. But even French sources did not always agree.

INTRODUCTION

FROM THE SEA

The U.S. Navy is once again talking of expeditionary warfare. Such expeditions are seen as a key to its role in the twenty-first century. Expeditions form an integral part of "From the Sea . . . ," reiterated in "Forward . . . From the Sea," the Navy's littoral warfare forward presence, crisis management, and battlespace dominance strategy. First enunciated in these two key naval white papers in the early 1990s, the expeditionary emphasis was developed further—more informally—in U.S. Admiral William A. Owens' fine book *High Seas: The Naval Passage to an Uncharted World* (Annapolis, Md.: Naval Institute Press, 1995), for instance. Admiral Owens was at the time of writing his book Vice Chairman of the Joint Chiefs of Staff.

Expeditionary warfare is nothing new, as Admiral Owens points out. Presenting it as the cornerstone of our twenty-first century naval strategy *is* revolutionary, again repeating the Admiral. In any case, we need to look closely at what it is we are talking about.

France organized such an expedition back in 1945–1946, at the close of World War II, to take back its Indo-Chinese patrimony.

The story of that expedition is one full of adventure, foul as well as brave deeds, and glory, as well as the seeds of ultimate disaster. It provides one good case study of what expeditions involve. One can always be more objective about others.

THE POST–COLD WAR ERA

In the post–Cold War Era—today—the possibility of large-scale military conflict between the superpowers has been replaced by the probability of a series of minor—and perhaps not so minor—regional ones. Many if not most of these will take place within reach of seaborne expeditionary forces. If history is any guide—and I obviously think it is—we will be there. Some of the time, anyway.

The Navy–Marine Corps team is the ideal instrument for U.S. use within this kind of political situation. In place of a system of rigid alliances, the team's flexibility permits selective, nonautomatic intervention, historically our preference in such matters.

Amphibious forces are an essential component of the ability to project power—influence—from the sea. An amphibious task force is essentially made up of three basic elements: the escorts, the amphibious shipping, and the landing force. For the United States that last element involves our amphibious warfare specialists—the Marines.

The Navy–Marine Corps team can itself contribute significantly to the assumably ongoing political process. If desired, an amphibious force can be sailed with great fanfare, publicly demonstrating both interest and will, reach and intent. On the other hand, a series of quiet sailings "on routine exercises," with the task force forming up out of sight of land, quietly, may have more effect, and leaves a government's options open. The force can then be purposely routed so as to be seen or not, as desired.

While at sea, the force can feint at several objectives, deciding on a specific one whenever it chooses. While on station, the force can loiter ("poise"), awaiting events. While poised, reconnaissance can update existing intelligence and keep track of enemy forces. Raids can test enemy defenses. If and when the decision to go in is made, the force can tailor the assault—using LCACs (landing craft, air cushion), helicopters and/or V-22s (Ospreys), and/or armored amphibious assault vehicles ("alligators")—to that specific objective. From the sea—afloat, offshore—will come the force's logistics, directly, as will its gunfire (artillery) support. Command, control, and communications for the overall force will remain afloat, too.

Once landed, the landing force can be left to finish the job by itself, whatever it is. Or it can be relieved by others, some or all of it pulled out to return to the poise or to feint—or immediately land—elsewhere. But things were not and probably will never always be quite like that—as is demonstrated in what follows—either for us, or others.

Let us note a couple of things before we start. In presenting the story of this expedition, I am not claiming that it represents an exact model for any of ours. God forbid that we should ever have to start as far behind the curve as the French here did! Please note. But there is nothing entirely new under the sun, and at some level there are ideas here that might be of use to us. Technical advances modify tactics long before they affect strategic ideas.

The last thing I wish to point out is the extreme politicization of small wars. The smaller the expedition—a division, a corps—the more politicized its operations become. Political advisors and civil affairs officers are acquiring roles lower down in expeditions than ever before, and important ones at that. It is more possible today than ever to win every military skirmish and never win the last battle. The French here showed us that.

FRENCH INDOCHINA

In this book, most of us are entering one of what are to us the far-off, strange, exotic lands east of Suez. To make much sense out of what here follows—to make your way along the tangled web of Indochina's immediate post–World War II history—it is necessary to begin at least with events that took place back in 1940. Even in this short book this we must also do.

French Indochina (*L'Union Indochinoise*) until 1945 was made up of five states (see Map I-1): the colony of Cochin-China and the protectorates of Tonkin, Annam, Cambodia, and Laos. Geographically, it consists of two large river deltas (the Mekong, politically Cochin-China and Cambodia; and the Red, or Rouge, Tonkin) held together by a jagged mountain backbone running the entire length of the country. The mountains (the *Chaine Annamite*) are a tumbled seven-thousand-foot range, with individual peaks reaching as high as ten thousand feet.

Indochina measures roughly 1,100 miles (1,800 kilometers) from the northernmost point on the Chinese border to Cape Camau in the south. Each delta is roughly 440 miles (700 kilometers) deep.

The whole of Indochina—the three Annamese Kys (the states of Cochin-China, Annam, and Tonkin) plus Laos and Cambodia—measured 272,360 square miles on which at this time lived some thirty million people. The three Kys alone take in 127,260 square miles, called home by some twenty-five million people, a little more than half in the north. The Annamese of the south carried a strong admixture of Cambodian blood in their veins; some Cham culture had followed the Mekong down, too. Those of the north showed a heavy Chinese strain, following the Red River down.

Graceful Saigon—the "Paris of the East"—on the Saigon River at the northeast corner of the Mekong Delta was the principal city of the south. Indochina's political, administrative, and industrial center—Hanoi, on the Red River—was the north's main city.

In 1940, there were perhaps fifty thousand French and colonial military personnel in Indochina, safeguarding the lines of communication, defending the borders, maintaining internal order for the thirty million civilians, including forty thousand Europeans. Not a lot.

Indochina has more than fifteen hundred miles of coastline, much of it rocky and dangerous for mariners. There are few good harbors. Nonetheless, some ninety percent of all transportation in 1945 was by water, along these coasts, up and down the sometimes difficult rivers and across the canals. There were few roads and fewer railroads—one Saigon-Hanoi, two from Hanoi north into

Map I-1
INDOCHINA

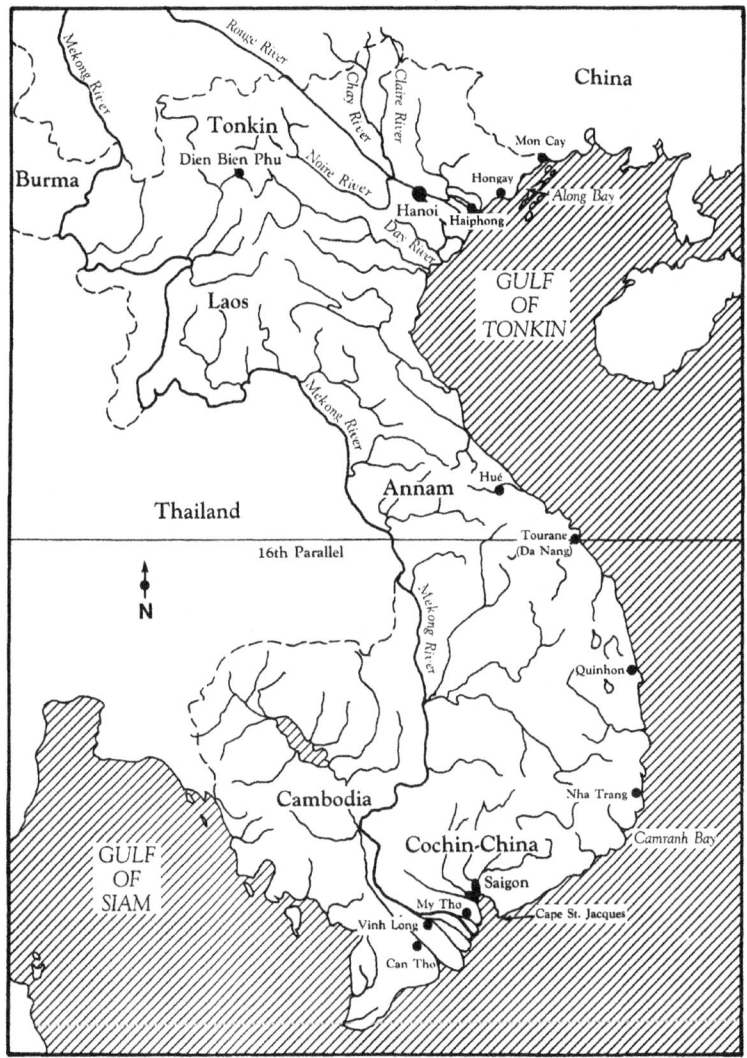

Indochina has two major river systems, that of the Rouge in the north and that of the Mekong on the south.

China. For the bulk of the people most of the time, the remainder of the country was effectively passable only on its waterways. France's principal Far Eastern naval base was itself in Indochina, at Saigon where there was a considerable naval arsenal. There was a secondary base (*point d'appui*) located at Haiphong. Camranh Bay was quasi-developed as another one. The naval air station was outside Saigon, at Cat-Lai.

THE VICHY YEARS

As a result of the total collapse of French ground and air forces in May and June of 1940 and the resulting Franco-German armistice, three-fifths of metropolitan France—Paris and the north and west coasts—was occupied by the Germans. The French Government fled Paris for Tours, Bordeaux, and finally Vichy, in the unoccupied zone. The colonies were left to France. Marshal Pétain was elected head of what government there was. France began damage control, to salvage what it could.

In London, an acting brigadier general named Charles de Gaulle refused to accept the armistice, setting up an organization he called "Fighting France" or "Free France," with the British as sponsors. Around him rallied an alternative to Vichy.

In Indochina, Vice Admiral Jean Decoux, commander of French Naval Forces, Far East (*Forces Navales d'Extrême-Orient*), was named Vichy's Governor General. Decoux moved to Hanoi, the colonial capital, leaving naval headquarters in Saigon. Neither Decoux nor Indochina ever rallied de Gaulle. London instituted an immediate blockade.

Submitting then to *force majeure*, the Allies then being unable to help him, Governor General Decoux was to negotiate a series of accords with Tokyo, regularizing a *modus vivendi* between them. Decoux, however, continued to govern Indochina. The tricolor continued to fly over the citadel at Hanoi. Japanese troops were stationed in Indochina until 1945; they did not occupy it, and they did not interfere with internal matters.

In 1940, in the first of the Hanoi-Tokyo accords, the Japanese

INTRODUCTION

gained the right to utilize ports and airfields in Tonkin, for use in their ongoing war with China. In 1941 the Japanese demanded and received further concessions. They moved into the south, into the harbors and airfields from which they later launched their operations against Malaya and the Netherlands East Indies.

In 1941 the Japanese gained the right to station forty thousand troops in Indochina. By 1945 these had grown to some sixty thousand, ten times the number agreed upon in 1940. They neglected to garrison the Paracel Islands just to the east, but they had occupied the Spratlies, three hundred miles to the southeast.

LA MARINE NATIONALE

Indochina being halfway around the world from France, everything then and later depended first of all on the French Navy. Paris historically maintained two levels of naval forces in the Far East: FNEO—*Forces Navales d'Extrême-Orient*—with overall strategic responsibility for defending French interests in the Pacific; and *Marine Indochine*, specifically responsible for the naval policing of Indochina. Even taken together, it was a small force. By December 1940 the principal elements of this combined force were as follows:

- light cruiser *Lamotte-Picquet* (a second, heavy cruiser—*Suffren*—had rallied Force X in Alexandria, Egypt)
- colonial gunboats (sloops) *Admiral-Charner, Dumont-d'Urville* (arrived in October)
- old sloops *Tahure* and *Marne*
- old small river gunboats (*Avalanche, Cdt-Bourdais, Vigilante, Mytho, Tourane*)
- hydrographic ships *Laperouse, Octant, Astrolabe*
- buoy tender *Armand-Rousseau*
- aircraft (eight flying boats)

Together with a heavily reinforced division-sized Army garrison and a small air force composed of obsolescent aircraft, they kept the peace.

With the armistice, all of Indochina—including the *Marine*—had been cut off from the *métropole*. From then on, there were no more reliefs of ships, no rotation of personnel, no replacements of or parts for equipment except for what could be run through the British blockade. Even that soon dried up.

By November 1942 only the colonial gunboat *Admiral-Charner*, the sloops *Marne* and *Tahure*, the five river gunboats, the three hydrographic ships, and the buoy tender remained active. *Lamotte-Picquet* was laid up for lack of replacement parts and the shortage of fuel oil.

It was this small force that escorted French convoys carrying the essential Indo-Chinese north-south trade, exchanging Tonkin's coal for Cochin-China's rice. It was this force that destroyed a hostile Thai Navy at Koh Chang in 1941. It was they who kept the watch along the coasts and on the rivers, maintaining order and enforcing law.

Defections, U.S. bombs, torpedoes, and mines, and just normal wear and tear ate at this isolated force until by 1945 there was very little left of the two cruisers, two colonial gunboats, two old sloops, five small river gunboats, three hydrographic vessels, and one buoy tender that it had had in 1940. In March the Japanese finished the job. More on this later.

PEACE?

France, like every other Western power, was caught absolutely unready by the suddenness of World War II's Pacific end. France's navy (*la Marine Nationale*) was indeed making a comeback. On V-E Day in Europe—in May 1945—the *Marine* consisted of an assortment of almost everything required for a balanced fleet: battleships, heavy cruisers, light cruisers (really large, fast destroyer-leaders), destroyers, and supporting craft.

But the *Marine* was an unbalanced force, heavy at the top. There were aircraft but no fighters. Its personnel were more than adequate, although their training was somewhat outdated. But above all, its metropolitan base structure, ravaged by the war, had been left a wreck.

During the last days of the war in Europe, a French naval task force had been assembled to clear the approaches to Bordeaux, still held by the Germans. The United States had to supply fuel, training facilities, a repair unit, aircraft, and twenty-four LCVPs to be manned by French crews before it could go to work.

THE FAR EAST

France had in fact already sent its only operational modern fast battleship—the new *Richelieu*—accompanied by one of the light cruisers—*Triomphant*—to Southeast Asia to serve under British command. But except for a Madagascar brigade, there were no sizable French troop units there. It was on this that Paris had to build.

When after V-J Day, Paris moved to reclaim its Southeast Asian possessions—Indochina, its South Pacific islands—it had no immediate means for doing so. In Indochina, a hostile communist-led local nationalist movement—the Viet-Minh—moved to fill the power void.

The British—charged under General Order No. 1 with overall Allied responsibility for law and order in the Southeast area—had their own hands full and could spare little for Indochina. Neither could the Dutch. The United States—strongly anticolonial—refused to help in any significant way. Our OSS, in fact, continued for a while to give the Viet-Minh limited support.

1

PROLOGUE: WORLD WAR II

ONE MORE TO GO—JAPAN

In the spring of 1945, in the east, the Americans were mopping up the Philippines. Except for the remaining what should have been relatively minor actions, their attention was being monopolized with preparations to invade the Japanese home islands themselves sometime later in the year. In the meantime, the Navy and the Air Force mined the Japanese in. These mines together with our submarines paralyzed Japan's sea communications in what amounted to a total blockade. The Air Force meantime firebombed the wood and paper Japanese cities one by one, burning them to heaps of ashes.

Nonetheless, the expected final battles on Japan's own soil indeed were seen to be furious ones. Iwo Jima and Okinawa were bad enough. Here in the east, the exultation of one victory was accompanied by a background dread of what was yet to come. But at least those battles would be the last ones.

We in the United States knew little and cared less about what was going on or was to take place in Indochina. We were in full cry now against the Japanese and meant to finish them off. All our energies were taken up with that, focused on the idea of Japan's unconditional surrender. Pearl Harbor would be avenged!

Beyond that, the average American seemingly had only a hazy idea that colonialism was immoral (we were in the process of turning the Philippines loose) and that most of the world's ills would disappear if all the countries became independent democracies, like ours. Some colonialisms were worse than others, however, and somehow President Franklin D. Roosevelt had decided that France's was among the bad ones. That idea would haunt us after he was gone.

Vice President Harry S. Truman became president in April 1945 when Roosevelt died. Vice presidents in the United States in those days had little to do with policy. Basically, Truman had to have spent the period covered in this book learning what was going on. In the meantime, he continued Roosevelt's policies, only modifying them as he found his way.

INDOCHINA

In Indochina, in Saigon at naval headquarters and at the cafés along the Rue Catinat, and in the citadel at Hanoi, it began to seem that under a skillful Decoux France might have pulled off the rationally impossible. Indochina still flew the tricolor. The image of a neutral Indochina, carefully honoring the Decoux accords of 1940–1941, had been kept. In August 1944, de Gaulle had even granted Decoux extraordinary powers, the better to cope with the uncertain days seen ahead. Decoux never got them.

De Gaulle had been attempting to establish contact with Decoux. In November 1944, Decoux was ordered to remain at his post, no matter what. Local feuds, however, prevented any real contact. Decoux remained at his post.

It began to appear to the French that the war might have bypassed them out here at the end of the world, the main battles taking place to the west, east, and northeast. Decoux was even considering means of offering himself as an intermediary between Japan and the Allies in Southeast Asia.

But as Allied victory began to seem inevitable, plans for a French anti-Japanese uprising began to form. Troops were placed on alert and moved to defensive positions throughout the country. Signs of a Gaullist underground began to appear. The Japanese could not but have noted this unaccustomed activity.

In November 1944 a French (Gaullist) military mission arrived in Ceylon, at Mountbatten's headquarters. The admiral accepted their credentials, ignoring whatever political implications that might have had. The French mission immediately began parachuting officers into Indochina to support the resistance nets.

The French were playing with fire in all this. The Allies were indeed driving toward victory, but they were still in no position to intervene effectively in Indochina should the Japanese move against the French. Decoux's neutrality was still their best defense. They were busy undermining that, now.

CRUMBLING EMPIRE

These increasingly apparent French attitudes and intentions, as well as outside events, put Tokyo on the alert. It followed with close attention as the French began to redeploy their troops, breaking up their large agglomerations into small units and sending them out into the country, to "sanctuaries," preferably in the mountains. These sanctuaries were occupied immediately in Tonkin, but only after alert in the south. Tokyo responded by building its effectives up to sixty thousand men and by matching each of the new positions with units of its own superior in numbers and arms.[1]

For these French moves to make military sense, they had to be part of a larger plan, one that included large-scale Allied landings on the coast. Despite the trumpetings by French radio of the imminence of such landings, the Allies had no such intentions. The British were totally committed, driving toward Singapore. So were the Americans, headed next for Okinawa, then Japan.

The Japanese cannot but have been of mixed minds about all this. Indochina—particularly Tonkin—had historically always been difficult to govern, but Tokyo needed a secure rear. Up until then, the French had supplied that. But underneath, Hanoi was seething with unrest. What would happen without Decoux? Letting the French govern for them had had its definite good points.

In 1940, Vichy had recognized Tokyo's "preeminent position" in the Far East. In 1941 Decoux had agreed that all rice, rubber, and coal that were normally exported were from then on to be reserved exclusively for Japan and its armed forces. Hanoi had fitted very nicely into Tokyo's Greater East Asia Co-Prosperity Sphere. Tokyo had once even come up with parts for the repair of cruiser *Lamotte-Picquet*'s boilers, available nowhere else. Without Decoux, the last vestiges of that relationship would be gone. Who knew what would come in its place?

DESTROYING THE BALANCE

In 1940 and 1941, France had had to accommodate to Japan. Alone, it had no hope of resisting Tokyo's demands. U.S. aid was asked, but there was none to be had. The 1940 accords between Japan and Vichy had given Tokyo the ability to cut off the flow of war materials to China via Haiphong and had given them access to Southern China via the Red River. The 1941 accords had given them the bases they needed for their coming drive to the south: airfields and port facilities at Tourane, Camranh, and Saigon. Now Tokyo's preeminent position was melting away.

U.S. aircraft stationed in southern China first bombed targets in Indochina in August 1942. Haiphong was targeted repeatedly, until by late 1944 Japanese ships appeared to be avoiding it entirely. Coastal shipping remained a priority target.

To the French, the situation by 1944 must have presented a great temptation. But the basic situation was unchanged. As things still were, in Indochina they were on their own. Alone, they could not resist Japanese demands, much less throw them out. France's remaining sovereignty rested on a position of equilibrium between the Japanese and the Chinese, only.

Then on January 12, 1945, a U.S. task group (Rear Admiral Gerald F. Bogan)—four carriers, two battleships, six cruisers, and twenty destroyers—struck the Indochina coast. In the course of this raid, the carriers' planes sank forty-four ships totaling 132,700 tons. Included in this total were fifteen combatant ships and twelve oil tankers. The Japanese lost a total of 110 planes in what was one of the heaviest blows to Japanese shipping in the war. This strike effectively put an end to major maritime traffic along the Indochina coast.

Much of the information on which this raid was based came from French Commander Robert Meynier's intelligence net. This net—port officials, lighthouse keepers, customs officers, and many others in Haiphong, Camranh, and Saigon—was apparently only one of several working there. Most were based in Kunming (China). *Japan's Kempetai* could not but know about them.

THE JAPANESE COUP

But then on March 9, 1945—the British in Burma and the United States just across the South China Sea in the Philippines—Imperial General Headquarters in Tokyo decided to seize full control of Indochina before the situation got out of hand. Outside events were tipping the scales.

Running through the South China Sea—between Indochina and the "dangerous ground" to the east—Japan's north-south sea lines of communication were now in danger of being cut. This would isolate the home islands from the resources and troops of the south. The uneasy Japanese denounced the 1940–1941 Decoux accords and in a brutal *coup de force* militarily took over the whole of Indochina. They installed a puppet Indo-Chinese government and prepared for defense. The Imperial Japanese Navy (IJN) did its bit.

In their coup, the Japanese eliminated the last major elements of Vichy's *Marine Indochine*. Its ships were either sunk by artillery fire from the shore, captured, or scuttled by their crews. Its personnel were made prisoner. One plucky colonial gunboat (sloop) attempted to run for the Philippines, but it was sunk by IJN aircraft off My-Tho.

In their coup, the Japanese destroyed more than half the French Indochina Army. Some five thousand troops under General Alessandri did fight their way out north into China. There Chunking promptly interned them.

The French had called on the Allies for help. The British managed to parachute in some arms—not many—but that was all. The United States refused all help. There was little to be had, in any case.

Some scattered small French Army and Navy units managed to rally the myriad, remote Fai-Tsi-Long Islands, which marked the eastern limits of Along Bay. In August these units passed under the orders of the French military mission in Kunming (Commandant Sainteny). There he integrated them in "Mission Maroc," a short-lived mixed Army-Navy team in which the Navy was charged with collection of intelligence, liaison, and transport of troops, all along Tonkin's northeast coast.

Decoux himself was of course arrested by the Japanese and held at tiny Loc-Ninh, 80 miles north of Saigon. His skillful, dogged five-year defense of French interests collapsed around him. Decoux was never to resume power. He deserved better than that. Once again, treason was a matter of geography.[2]

PLANS FOR THE EAST

By 1945, there were in the East two major Allied commands. U.S. Admiral Chester Nimitz ran the Pacific war from headquarters in Hawaii. Britain's Admiral Lord Louis Mountbatten ran Southeast Asia from Ceylon. It was Admiral Mountbatten's command that most affected our story, but the United States and China played their part, too. At least at first. Events were to catch all of them up short.

As late as mid-1945, in the Eastern Theater—in the Pacific, in China, and in Southeast Asia—what plans for the war there were dealt mainly with the coming invasion of the still-intact Japanese homeland. Beyond that, it was expected that the slow, deliberate mopping up of Southeast Asia, the Philippines, and China would continue as the colonial powers—Britain, the Netherlands,

France—moved to reclaim their lost territories and the United States to keep its promises. Little more.

Under the circumstances, it was foregone that Britain would be the ultimate organizer for postwar restoration of colonial authority in Southeast Asia. Allied General Order No. 1—drafted by the U.S.—confirmed this. Britain itself, however, had its hands full with India, Burma, and Malaya. The Dutch could spare very little from the difficult cleanup of the Netherlands East Indies. Both were to contribute what they could. In any case, France's prewar colonial system was a tightly closed one. Except for the example Indochina set, there was not a lot of basic Allied interest in recovering it.

With victory in Europe, major additional increments of military power began to arrive in the East, shifted from Europe. But at Headquarters, Supreme Allied Commander Southeast Asia (Admiral Lord Louis Mountbatten) on Ceylon, V-J Day was not seen as coming anytime soon.

Only at the Potsdam summit in July was any agreement even in bare principle reached on post V-J Day plans. With peace in the East, the British would be directly responsible for reoccupying the southern half of Indochina, up to the 16th parallel of latitude. The Nationalist (Chunking or Kuomintang) Chinese would be responsible for occupying the north. The French were not even mentioned in all this. They would have to work things out with the British.

The division of Indochina at the 16th parallel coincided with nothing geographic, political, economic, or social. It just arbitrarily cut the country across the middle of Annam, the central Ky. Division here had originally been designed to protect China's right and Britain's left flank during the coming fighting with Japan, but that was of course no longer valid. Everyone was just stuck with the line.[3]

CARVING A ROLE

With peace in Europe, France had in some respects reverted to the role it had held since the 1940 armistice: the uninvited at the party. U.S. President Roosevelt had gone on record that the United

States would not assist European powers recover their lost colonies. This included France. But with or without outside help, Paris had to act. Indochina was Paris's window on the Pacific—and major symbol of France's importance in the world, still. But what could Paris do in the meantime? There was still work to be done. Discussions between French Vice Admiral Raymon Fenard, chief of their naval mission in Washington, and the Anglo-American Combined Chiefs of Staff (CCS) led to the following agreement in principle:

- The CCS accepted the participation of the French Navy in the Pacific war, except for the French naval air arm.
- The French ships sent were to be integrated within Allied tactical groups.
- The French contribution was to be made battle-ready by the French themselves.

Individual French ships had been fighting in the Far East with the Allies since 1943 and were still there. But the Paris Government was now determined to participate with a recognizable French fleet. On this basis, in July plans were finalized. They provided for the contribution for the Far East—when ready—of the following, to serve together as a unit:

- New fast battleship *Richelieu* and large destroyer-leader (she was called a light cruiser, now) *Triomphant*, already on-scene
- Four cruisers, two more destroyer-leaders, and twenty-five smaller combatants
- A fleet train
- A naval infantry brigade, to fight ashore

As can be seen, there was no provision for any aircraft carrier, no organic aviation, no amphibious capability at all. But events overtook these plans even before they were really put into motion back home.[4]

V-J DAY

By the summer of 1945, the Japanese naval and merchant fleets gone, traffic even on the Inland Sea paralysed, our Third Fleet and Air Force increasing daily the tempo of their strikes against the home islands, American forces were being gathered for the final amphibious assaults. Certain elements in Tokyo were in fact investigating the terms that Washington might demand in a negotiated peace. The Pacific war was undoubtedly drawing to a close, but the French—like everyone else—thought that there was time enough to fill in these plans.

The Three Power Alliance (the United States, Britain, and China) had set forth at Potsdam its Japanese surrender terms. But nothing had been heard from Tokyo, where violent argument still raged. Then with almost incredible suddenness—unexpected to all but the very few top Allied leaders in the know—two atomic bombs were dropped by the United States on an already collapsing homeland Japan. Hiroshima was hit August 6, Nagasaki on the 9th. Tokyo sued for peace.

On August 14, 1945, the war in the Pacific was over. Not one of the French, especially, had had any inkling of what was afoot, but V-J Day was here! No one however—not even the Americans—was really ready for it. Ready or not, peace was here!

But what a peace!

NOTES

1. Paul Auphan and Jacques Mordal, *La Marine Française dans la Seconde Guerre Mondiale* (Paris: Editions France-Empire, 1976), passim; Henri Darrieus and Jean Quéguiner, *Historique de la Marine Française* (Novembre 1942–Août 1945), (Saint-Malo: Editions l'Ancre de Marine, 1994), p. 318.

2. Jean Decoux, *A la barre de l'Indochine* (Paris: Plon, 1949), passim;

Paul Romé, *Les Oubliés du Bout du Monde* (Paris: Editions Maritimes & d'Outre-Mer, 1983), passim.

3. Edwin Bickford Hooper, Dean C. Allard, and Oscar P. Fitzgerald, *The United States Navy and the Vietnam Conflict: The Setting of the Stage to 1959* (Washington, D.C.: Naval History Division, 1976), pp. 87–88.

4. Auphan and Mordal, passim; Jean Gabrié, *Les Marines de la Guerre 1935–1945* (Vincennes: Service Historique de la Marine, 1994), p. 107.

2

THE EXPEDITION IS FORMED

REACTION IN CEYLON

At Admiral Mountbatten's headquarters in Ceylon, the staff was caught as short as anywhere else. Mountbatten was faced with now disarming the Japanese troops, sending them home, and at the same time restoring legitimate government to a far-flung area that included Burma, Thailand (Siam), Southern Indochina, as well as Malaya, Singapore, and Indonesia. Most of it was colonial, a treasured part of the British, French, and Dutch empires. The whole area was in any case in turmoil, with collaborators and nationalists on every hand, some in effective control, arming themselves with whatever they could get their hands on.

No one knew for sure what to expect now from the various Japanese occupying units. Their armed forces historically were unruly, units sometimes refusing orders from higher commands, acting instead on their own. There were even rumors of a military *coup d'état* in Tokyo, so as to continue the war. Security would have to continue to be an important factor in whatever the Allies now did. So would "face," always important in the East, but doubly so for the returning colonial powers. After all, they still carried the burden of previous, repeated humiliations and defeats. Full ceremony to emphasize the various local Japanese surrenders was called for, even demanded.

So in spite of the formal cease-fire—fearful of local Japanese response—Admiral Mountbatten's reaction to events was to order his forces to carry out previously planned landings in Indonesia and Malaya, at once, ready for anything. His Eastern Fleet's Force 62 (battleships *Nelson* [flag] and *Richelieu*, two cruisers, *Triomphant*, and eleven destroyers) supported landings at Penang (September 2) and Singapore (September 12). There was in fact no resistance at all.

From Singapore, Indochina lay only some six hundred miles northeast across the South China Sea. With all the intelligence agencies that were operating in Indochina, there must have been reports about what was happening there. It must have been very difficult for the French ships to now return to base, as ordered. Return they did.[1]

PARIS'S ATTITUDE

The Gaullists were in power now in Paris. Charles de Gaulle was himself chief of the provisional government. Vichy was no more. Pétain was under arrest. It was the Gaullist vision of the future that would determine Paris's attitude toward events in Indochina now. They had one ready. Indeed they did—a rational, just one.

Japan's sudden and complete cessation of resistance left the Allies with hopes that their return would be an orderly, easy one, everywhere. That was not to be. Far from it.

The initial Allied landings were—and could only be—token ones. Under the armistice, the Japanese were everywhere to keep order until relieved. They would then be disarmed and returned home. Rather, the Allies found that the Japanese had already unleashed a nationalist whirlwind everywhere.

The prewar French empire was a highly centralized affair, as was France itself. But now everywhere colonies were talking of some

THE EXPEDITION IS FORMED 23

measure of self-government, even of independence. This included the average Annamese, the *nha-qué*.

Now, Indochina was being offered considerable self-rule in domestic affairs. The Gaullist Free French movement drew its original geographic support from the fringes of France's empire, principally those in Central Africa. De Gaulle was quite aware of the growing national aspirations of those colonies. In December 1943 de Gaulle had issued his Brazzaville Declaration. In it the French community became a French Union. In it he promised postwar Indochina—within a federal organization—all of the attributes of a free state.

The Brazzaville Declaration was reinforced by another issued in March 1945, this time in Paris, directed specifically at Indochina. This one spelled out—still within the overall French Union—an Indo-Chinese Federation. This federation was to continue to have a French governor general but also an Indo-Chinese assembly and a mixed council of state. Its exterior interests were to be represented by France, as before.[2]

How could any reasonable man say no to this?

This all may not sound like very much, but de Gaulle's plan was—for the French—quite a progressive one. Within a federated Indochina, the plan provided for free elections for the first time. Except that within the British Commonwealth the Governor General or Viceroy had become more and more only a figurehead, the Commonwealth and the French Union looked a lot alike.

PARIS'S EXPEDITION

Japan's surrender on August 14 completely transformed the projected French contribution to the Pacific war. Within the framework laid down, Paris's project became an expedition. The task of the *Marine Nationale* from then on was no longer to participate in a major war. It was rather to transport to the Far East as rapidly as possible—and support—the forces necessary for the reassertion of French sovereignty in Indochina, a colony still occupied for the most part by Japanese troops and falling into chaos.

Technically, the projected fleet became part of what was now loosely called the *Corps Expeditionnaire d'Extrême-Orient* (CEEO), or Far East Expeditionary Corps. There were other internal changes, too. CEEO was ground forces-heavy, now.

To reassert French sovereignty, reestablish law and order, relieve the British and Chinese, building on the previous only half-formed plans, Paris was able to assign some of the best key personnel it had. Passionate Gaullist Vice Admiral Georges Thierry d'Argenlieu was appointed High Commissioner, with both political and military powers. Army Lieutenant General Jacques-Philippe de Hautecloque (called Leclerc)—authentic hero of North Africa and Europe—was named commanding general, Genesuper under d'Argenlieu.

General Leclerc's troop list included the following:

- The Far East Expeditionary Corps itself—an Army corps of two colonial infantry divisions and one armored division (Leclerc's old 2nd Armored)—from the *métropole*
- An independent colonial brigade, based in Madagascar
- Reconstituted units salvaged from various troops already in the area
- The reorganized Far East Naval Forces
- The air elements present in the Far East

The Army corps gave its name loosely to the entire force, as we said.

Admiral d'Argenlieu arrived in Ceylon on September 10. There reportedly was not room for both d'Argenlieu and Leclerc (or really was it Mountbatten?) in Ceylon. D'Argenlieu left at once for Chandernagor (India) where he made his headquarters and where he gathered the reins of what was going on in Indochina into his hands. D'Argenlieu was to make his appearance in Saigon only on October 30. A curious delay this was.

General Leclerc on the other hand arrived in Ceylon August 22. There and from there he acted as d'Argenlieu's advance agent throughout the Far East. It was he who represented France at General MacArthur's ceremonial staging of the surrender of Japan itself, on board the U.S. battleship *Missouri* in Tokyo Bay on September 2. On his way back south, he stopped off at Manila for conversations with MacArthur's staff. Leclerc took command of CEEO in Saigon on October 5. Leclerc left tracks all over.

In the midst of all this, the general commanding his Army corps died. Leclerc took over direct command of the corps, too.

FNEO RECONSTITUTED

The Far East Naval Forces (FNEO) were in turn commanded by Vice Admiral Philippe-Marie-Joseph-Raymond Auboyneau, also of Free French fame. FNEO was an overall organization, like CEEO, itself made up of five subordinate elements. Building on previous plans, Paris was able to commit the following naval elements for service in the Far East. Their content—together with dates of availability in Toulon—is described here:

- **FNEO**, the theater-level element (Vice Admiral Auboyneau): one battleship and one destroyer-leader (already in place); a cruiser (September 15); another destroyer-leader (September 5); and a sloop (October 5). This was "the fleet."

  FNEO was given the task of cooperating with ground and air forces in reestablishing French interests in the Far East, particularly in Indochina.

  In employing the forces placed under his orders, Auboyneau would receive his directives from the commander-in-chief. With this reservation, Auboyneau exercised all the attributions of the commander of an independent naval force.

- **Marine Indochine** (Rear Admiral Gaston-Elie Graziani): three sloops and a destroyer (all by September 15); plus two more destroyers (later, no date). These were "district forces."

Graziani had the task of contributing to the reestablishment of French sovereignty in Indochina and of returning its naval infrastructure to an operational state.

- **A transport force**: two old cruisers (September 15) with two more December 1; plus an aircraft transport, two auxiliary cruisers, an oiler, and a repair ship (as ready).
  The Navy alone could provide transport quickly. Air transport on this scale was not to be had. Merchant transports were still controlled by the Allied shipping pool and were not at French call. The Navy had to take this on.

- **An Aéronavale** (naval air arm) **group**: one eight-plane Catalina PBY squadron together with a mobile air base to be brought in on the aircraft transport.

- **Brigade Marine d'Extrême-Orient (BMEO)**, or Far East Naval Brigade: these were *Fusiliers Marins*, naval infantry (or Marines) attached to Leclerc's army corps.[3]

LIMITATIONS

Altogether, this represented a not inconsiderable force. There again was France's new fast battleship *Richelieu*. There were the cruisers *Emile-Bertin, Suffren, Gloire, Tourville*, and *Duquesne* and the destroyer-leaders *Fantasque* and *Triomphant*. There were the destroyers (ex-U.S. destroyer escorts) *Somali, Sénégalais, Algérien*. The colonial gunboat *Savorgnan-de-Brazza*, also included, was rated a sloop. There were the sloops *Annamite, Chevreuil*, and *Gazelle*. There was the force train and BMEO.

All of the world's major navies—those that had fought all through the whole of World War II—looked a lot different at the end. The aircraft carrier and its aircraft had replaced the battleships as the centerpiece of fleets, as everyone knows. Battleships had been relegated to antiaircraft escorts for the carriers or to providing shore gunfire support. There were much higher proportions of destroyers and of ASW craft. All had developed a significant capability for amphibious assault of a hostile shore.

More had changed during World War II, missed by most of the *Marine*. VHF and UHF radio had arrived. Radar had transformed navigation, maneuver, and gunfire control. Sonar had done the same for ASW. AA defense had been developed, especially against close-in, low-flying planes. Naval aircraft—for reconnaissance, patrol, defense, and strike—had come of age. So had landing ships and craft.

The overall relationship between the Allies and the French *Marine* was governed between 1943 and 1945 by the Anglo-American Combined Chiefs of Staff (CCS) already mentioned, through a document eventually called CCS 358. Under it the Allies assisted the recovery of the battered *Marine*, but only insofar as this help benefited the ongoing joint war effort.

Landing ships and craft were all specialized bow-ramped, beaching types. Landing ships were expected to operate shore to shore, carrying more, and were therefore larger. Landing craft were smaller, expected to operate ship to shore. They both ran to scores of subtypes, especially the landing craft, and could differ markedly between navies.

CEEO had none of these. For expediency as well as prestige, the French had concentrated on surface combatants, patrol, ASW, escort, and gunfire support. These the Allies could use and would back. Amphibious warfare was a complicated affair. It the Allies already had in hand.

AMPHIBIOUS CAPABILITY

In Indochina in 1945, Paris did not expect Leclerc's CEEO to have to execute an opposed landing, wherever he came ashore. All that should have been involved for CEEO initially was an administrative delivery of troops to ports already secured by the British and Chinese and their relief. Formal, technical amphibious capability in CEEO was therefore nonexistent. Apparently no real attempt was made to get any. There were still no assault transports, no landing ships or craft.

In CEEO, there were, however, two important available sources of at least latent amphibious capability. These would both be called upon, in ways we recount as the story develops.

Today it may seem a little strange to us. We are all technicians too expensive to waste, and too few. But in the *Marine* of 1945, battleships and cruisers were still expected to be able to field a traditional landing party—made up from the crew—if called upon. For a battleship, these would be about 260 officers and men strong, for cruisers about half that. There was thus always a latent if crude amphibious capability in the force.

BMEO was expected to fight ashore as a regimental combat team—as integrated infantry, tanks, and artillery—as the *Fusilier Marins* under Leclerc in Europe, attached to the Army, had done. The *Fusiliers*, however, were naval personnel commanded by line naval officers. There was thus always a latent amphibious capability here, too.

DIPLOMATIC PRELIMINARIES

For France, there were still diplomatic preliminaries to be gone through. The Allies had to be kept informed. Most of the *Marine Nationale*'s best ships were tied up, committed to Allied tasks. The British supported some of them, under the terms of a document called AFN 1. Paris had to regain control of its fleet first.

Having waited a decent interval so as not to upstage MacArthur's ceremony, on the 12th Mountbatten held his own formal surrender of Japanese forces in Southeast Asia, in Singapore. This was quite a production, staged with all the grandeur of empire.

In Singapore the high point was when, in an apparently endless file, several hundred Japanese general and senior officers stepped forward to place their swords at the foot of Mountbatten's tribune. For a samurai there could be no greater shame. For watching Southeast Asia, the lesson was plain. Britain had won. *Richelieu*'s Captain Merveilleux du Vignaux was present, leading a detachment of his crew, at the affair. So was Leclerc.[4]

CABBAGES AND KINGS

According to previous agreements, initial logistic support for CEEO was to be provided by the British. But on September 2, Mountbatten made it known that, aside from *Richelieu* and *Triomphant*, he would not be able to guarantee the support of any French units in Saigon before October 20. On September 5 and 6, therefore, Franco-British staff talks were held in Paris. Out of these talks came AFN 2, the document that guided British support for CEEO from then on.

There is a shabby counterpoint to all this. We all know about the gratitude of kings. Superceded, isolated, Admiral Decoux quit Indochina by plane, headed home. When Decoux stopped over in Calcutta, d'Argenlieu refused to meet him, sending him on to Paris. For four tense, difficult years, Decoux had held *la barre de l'Indochine* (Indochina's helm) with courage and dignity, against all winds and tides, and merited being treated with honor.

Arrested on his arrival in France, Decoux was imprisoned in the notorious Val de Grace for two years, awaiting trial. Investigation was unable to turn up anything against him, however. After all, his appointment as Governor General had been confirmed by de Gaulle as late as August 1944.

Forgotten at the end of the world, *les anciens* did not understand any of this, especially what Paris was up to, and they never forgave d'Argenlieu his bad manners.[5] But the damage had been done. The wonder was, when Paris again needed them they again answered its call. *La Royale*, as the French called it, was.

NOTES

1. Jean Gabrié, *Les Marines de la Guerre 1935–1945* (Vincennes: Service Historique de la Marine, 1994), pp. 108–9.
2. Georges Thierry d'Argenlieu, *Chronique d'Indochine 1945–1947* (Paris: Editions Albin Michel, 1985), passim.
3. Gabrié, pp. 109–10.

4. Henri Darrieus and Jean Quéguiner, *Historique de la Marine Française* (Novembre 1942–Août 1945), (Saint-Malo: Editions l'Ancre de Marine, 1994), pp. 224–25.

5. Paul Romé, *Les Oubliés du Bout du Monde* (Paris: Editions Maritimes & d'Outre-Mer, 1983), pp. 192–94.

3

THE PROBLEM

THE VIET-MINH (HO AND GIAP)

Facing High Commissioner Thierry d'Argenlieu and his military commander Leclerc was one basic problem and a collection of smaller ones. The basic problem was the Viet-Minh, a political coalition led by a small, thin Annamese communist named Ho Chi Minh and his military commander Vo Nguyen Giap. These communists were a small, tight group, hard-core types who had been fighting, losing, and learning all their lives.

Ho Chi Minh's basic task everywhere was to separate the people from the (legitimate) French colonial government at the point of contact and to substitute his own therefore. Though the communists were few, nationalists were, relatively speaking, many. The Viets adopted a nationalist stance.[1]

In August 1945 in Vietnam, there were six recognizable nationalist political parties as well as a score of independent nationalist politicians. They were ripe for the picking. The Viets, through temporary coalitions of expediency with even moderate nationalists, captured them and used them for their own purposes. Those groups and individuals they could not dominate they ruthlessly discredited. Individuals they terrorized, killed, or kidnapped, right from the beginning and without letup, no matter what the tactical relationship at the time.

Evidently the rebels had a program, they were ready, and they went right at it. Against them, the still organizing and unready nationalists had no chance. One by one, all opposition—even potential—either got in line or disappeared from the stage.

Outside powers helped them. Chiang Kai-shek had allowed Ho to base himself in Yunan, in south China. Ho had even received a little qualified support from Chiang. Chiang was wary, however; he had worked with communists before. Nonetheless, Ho thus became strongest in north Indochina, in Tonkin. From there, he reached south.

The United States helped him, with advisors and a few light arms. Our role, however, here appears sometimes to be overstated. We had other fish to fry. But in exchange the OSS did keep an eye on what was going on. Ho kept them on a short leash.

REACHING FOR POWER—THE "AUGUST UPRISING"

Peace or not, defeated or not, from mid-August to mid-September 1945 the occupying Japanese remained in effective control of Indochina. Their puppet government proved totally unable to govern and faded away. Before any of the Allies could organize themselves, the Japanese allowed the Viets to set up the beginnings of a de facto government of their own for the entire country. Ho started with a *fait accompli*, an advantage shared by few others like him. Sometimes overt, sometimes covert, it was never destroyed after that.

It was in August 1945, while the United States beat Japan into submission and the great powers maneuvered and held parades, that Ho Chi Minh reached this time for power. On the 7th at Hanoi the Viet-Minh boldly created the Committee for the Liberation of Vietnam. On the 8th at Saigon the Executive Committee of Nam-Bo was created. Viet-Minh assault squads occupied Hanoi's public buildings on the 18th. Ho proclaimed the establishment of a Democratic Republic of Vietnam the following day.

By the first week of September, then, Ho Chi Minh was in Hanoi, leading a communist-dominated coalition of nationalist parties. There he had set up the Vietnamese Democratic Republic—taking in all three Annamese Kys—Tonkin, Annam, and Cochin-China—with Hanoi as its capital, all with perhaps, ten thousand men.

Thus at the end Tokyo had its revenge. The already-defeated Japanese left d'Argenlieu the task of reconquering a people who had already been permitted their political freedom. To complicate the problem, local Japanese units furnished the Viets deserters, officers, and arms. Of the legitimate colonial government there was yet no sign.

THE COLONIAL IMAGE

The developing struggle between the French and the Viet-Minh was in essence for control of the bulk of the people, but only the French made any attempt to play by any kind of rules. In July 1945 a Japanese opinion poll—Japanese, and therefore under the circumstances to be believed—was taken in the Nha-Trang area. The poll revealed that 74 percent of the *nha-qués* remained pro-French. Those anti-French totaled no more than 14 percent.[2] Nationalism indeed was running through Southeast Asia like wildfire, but that evidently did not require that one be anti-French. This Ho Chi Minh had to change.

But as the legitimate colonial government began to return, these people were treated to the spectacle of discord among the French. With Gaullist versus Vichyite, it was for a while Frenchman versus Frenchman. Their colonial masters were in disarray, themselves divided. The Viets had no such problem. As the French washed their dirty linen, the Viets exploited it.

Mass reprisals, individual murder, rape, torture, pillage, and fire were the mark of the Viets, right from the first. They were used as a conscious political tool. They helped isolate the French and their local—if sometimes conditional—allies. These last included town mayors, administrators, village "notables" (traditional leaders), Catholic priests, merchants who refused to pay Viet taxes, newspaper editors, school teachers, the French military, the police, even those peasants who refused to serve in the Viet army or to inform on others.

Such behavior helped further destroy the myth of the superiority of both the Europeans and those who had adopted their ways. It vented desires for personal revenge. It bound even those who only watched passively more tightly to the rebel cause. Somehow they all became guilty. In this war, bystanders could not be innocent. As far as the Viets were concerned, those who were not with them were against them.

AGGRAVATING THE SITUATION

The basic, primary function of a government is to provide safety and security to its people. Because this is so, the Annamese had to be shown that only the Viet-Minh could provide this against the Viets. The French had to be shown unable to do so; they must rather be goaded into mindless reprisals against, and endless harassment of, the people.

Providing for the well-being of its people being the next most important function of government, the maximum of economic disorder had to be created. Strikes and sabotage became basic tools of the Viets. Public services were paralyzed. Plantations and factories were burned. Trade was brought to a halt, unless it produced taxes for the Viets, and perhaps even then.

Participation being the ultimate goal of a people—and with nationalism setting the developing world aflame—any future colonial government would have to provide this for Vietnam. De Gaulle's French Union would go a long way toward satisfying that need—and it could have been developed further, with time—given its chance. The French could not have that chance.

The French response to the Viet-Minh's "August Uprising" (the Viets wanted to tag it as a mass affair) had to be two-pronged. It

THE PROBLEM 35

would have to include a military facet, to gain the setting (order) and the time in which to negotiate an outline of the colony's future. It would have to include a political facet, too, an inevitable political compromise, acceptable to most people. There were hard-liners—even fanatics—on both sides. These last included the Viets—communist to the core—although they adopted a reasonable front easily enough whenever the tactic suited them. The French were to try both approaches, but the time available for them to work was short.

MORE AGGRAVATION

But to the basic problem of Ho, Giap, and their Viets must be added a number of immediate, more practical problems Paris had to face. Each one by itself alone would have been sufficient to justify a significant delay in Paris's response. But little could be done about these, in the end. Paris nonetheless achieved prodigies of improvisation, in spite of all.

Even after supporting Mountbatten's immediate post–cease-fire landings at Singapore and Penang, *Richelieu* and her consort were not released to French control. In the absence of instructions to the contrary, both were ordered to return to Ceylon with the rest of the fleet. Only then were they let go.[3]

In any case, General MacArthur—he understood the East—had insisted that there be no more local initiatives until there was a carefully staged formal overall surrender by Tokyo. As a result of various contretemps, this did not take place until September 2 in Tokyo Bay. Only then could serious recovery efforts begin. In the meantime the Japanese remained charged with maintaining order in the occupied lands.

FRENCH ASSETS

To make things worse, the various elements earmarked for CEEO were scattered widely, some in France and North Africa, others in Ceylon, Madagascar, China, and even the United States.

Their assembly would take time, even under the best of conditions. Some units and ships were in fact ready. Others were not. Some were even in the process of formation or refit. Staff work of the highest order was demanded now.

There remained the not inconsiderable but divided remnants of the old pre-collapse French units—*les Anciens d'Indochine*. Some were detained in Yunan, prisoners under Chinese guard. Others were imprisoned in Saigon and Hanoi under first Japanese, then Viet guard. Those in Saigon at least, all forty-five hundred of them, were packed together in an old regimental casern, ill-fed and abused. There were forty-five hundred more in Hanoi. Apparently, there were another twenty-five hundred in Haiphong.

Those imprisoned old Indochina hands (*les anciens*) were from Vichy units, however—suspected fascists per se in the eyes of the new political masters in Paris. About *les anciens*, everyone was receiving mixed signals, so no one did anything about them. They could have been a valuable immediate asset, if re-formed and re-armed, ready on the ground. They remained behind wire.

So while *Richelieu* and her consort waited in Ceylon for release by the British, Paris had to assemble the other ships, get some of them new crews, even a hull cleaning and a quick refit on the way, load them with whatever troops and equipment were ready, and send them out. Inescapably this all took time, something Paris just did not have very much of.

THE SCHISM

Not everything was even that simple, however. Not at all! Latent in the *Marine Nationale* at this point was a special trap: Its personnel were divided sharply in two. There were those of the regular French Navy, who had throughout the war stood by their oath of obedience, who had done their duty to the end. These were by far the majority. *Vichyites* they were tagged.

There were also the Gaullists, now integrated but considered renegades by the regulars, but who were in control, filling most of the key positions, one or sometimes two ranks above those held

THE PROBLEM

by their classmates. The wounds were still open. The Gaullists were not always tactful about it, either. During the war, the regulars had gone out of their way to avoid civil war, Frenchmen fighting each other. The Gaullists were never so tender-minded, pushing against that threshold in West Africa, in Djibouti, and in Syria.

The *Marine* in 1945 was actually in the midst of a Gaullist purge of its personnel, carried out in part by a board on which sat a noted communist, a Black Sea mutineer of twenty-five years earlier.[4] Schism there was in the "Grand Corps."

But the *Marine* was not known as *la Royale* for nothing. It soon absorbed the purge. Much damage was done, and many wrongs were inflicted, but the Grand Corps was a tightly knit one. Indochina gave it purpose again—at least that.

HURRY, HURRY

Meantime in Indochina, the fundamentally hostile communist-led Viet-Minh was steadily working to seize this once-in-a-lifetime opportunity, to themselves fill the political power void. As its enemies' heads were found on stakes in the village square, it grew stronger every day. Sabotage increased. Opposition disappeared. The mob was kept on the boil.

On September 2 in Saigon, to celebrate their independence, the local Viets (the "Nam-Bo") organized a parade through Saigon's European quarter. The Viets began by leading the mob around the casern, jeering at the POWs. It then turned the mob loose on the homes of well-known French civilians, finishing by pillaging the entire area, beating the men, raping the women, abusing the children. The Japanese watched.[5]

Ships now were sent on their way east as soon as ready for sea, in whatever order, each one carrying the maximum of troops. With the *métropole* itself still recovering from the aftermath of the war, it must have been a logistician's nightmare.

Béarn loaded 400 men, 215 vehicles, 9 LCVPs and 150 tons of food, and left; *Gloire*, 330 troops; *Suffren*, 450 troops and 130 naval personnel; *Ville de Strasbourg*, 166 *Fusiliers* plus matériel; *Quercy*, 283 men, 600 tons of matériel and food.

BMEO was, for instance, at the *Fusilier* base at Arcachon in the midst of organization and equipment. Being put together out of twenty-five hundred men from two regiments that had released their reservists, it was short of a number of technical personnel. They had to be found—and were.

MINES

Everybody had laid mines in Indo-Chinese waters. The French themselves had laid defensive fields, as did the Japanese IJN. The Americans and British laid offensive fields. The Japanese laid one 480-mine field off the entrance to Camranh, in October and December 1941. They laid the other 30-mine field off Poulo Cecir de Mer, just to the south, in May 1945. Between October 1942 and May 1945, the United States laid a total of some 550 mines, using both submarines and aircraft. The British laid more, using B-29s borrowed from the United States.

Saigon and Haiphong—the port for Hanoi—had both been mined. The *Marine* had managed to keep Saigon open, but Haiphong had been closed to deep-draft traffic, blocked by mines and sunken ships. The Japanese had lost a probable six ships totaling 10,460 tons to Allied mines, with an additional two (6,000 tons) damaged. The French lost perhaps six.

In no case, however, was local traffic—largely carried on small, wooden-hulled junks and sampans—appreciably affected. This continued to the end and beyond. Unless they actually hit a contact mine, they could be little hurt. They were much too shallow-drafted for there to be much chance of that.

WHERE TO HEAD?

The question of what port or ports the CEEO should make was being worked out even as it was being organized and sent on its way. Geography decreed that control of Indochina's two deltas

(Mekong, Red River) meant domination of the country. Saigon led to the first. Hanoi—through Haiphong—gained entrance to the second. Should it be one of these? Both?

Partly because of the mines, it was soon determined that, at this point, nothing could be done about returning to Hanoi. But also, beginning in early September, as settled at Potsdam, some 180,000 Chinese troops had moved in north of the 16th parallel. They were in part American-equipped, having come in from Burma. Chunking was quite obviously not interested in pulling them back out until the situation in the Far East had worked further out. In the meantime, as far as Chunking was concerned, the troops were no burden, living better than they would at home. That settled it. Hanoi would have to wait.

The British, however, sent a force to Saigon at the same time, as agreed. There was a firm understanding that CEEO would take over here as soon as it was strong enough on the ground to do so. Saigon thus became CEEO's initial port of entry.

THE U.S. POSITION

President Roosevelt, until he died in April 1945, then President Truman each resisted getting involved in any military effort toward the liberation of Indochina. The U.S. State Department's European Desk, on the other hand, strongly supported assisting France in this. On Indochina, it was overruled. Colonialism was immoral.

U.S. policy remained not to assist the French. To underscore its position, the United States publicly announced that it had withdrawn from Mountbatten's Southeast Asia command. It would provide no arms, ammunition, or landing craft. The employment of American ships to transport troops to Indochina was also barred. The British felt no such constraint.

Even though U.S. naval aid was for the same reason denied the *Marine*, France in this time did send out U.S.-built ships we provided them during the war, as well as French-built ones we had repaired and rebuilt in our yards. The former category apparently included three destroyer escorts and five minesweepers, nothing huge. The latter included *Richelieu, Béarn*, at least some of the cruisers, and two of the destroyer-leaders. A number of landing craft we had left behind were apparently picked up in Manila. In September 1945, France requested minesweepers to clear Indo-Chinese ports. U.S. naval authorities responded by suggesting that the request be resubmitted through diplomatic channels. That killed that. Some were even our mines! We had planted half of them![6]

NOTES

1. Roger Trinquier, *Modern Warfare* (New York: Praeger, 1964), passim.
2. Paul Romé, *Les Oubliés du Bout du Monde* (Paris: Editions Maritimes & d'Outre-Mer, 1983), p. 192n.
3. Bernard Favin-Lévêque, *Souvenirs de Mer et d'Ailleurs* (Versailles: Editions des 7 Vents, 1990), pp. 119–21.
4. Romé, passim, especially pp. 213–15; Favin-Lévêque, p. 127.

The communist in question was Charles Tillon, former naval quarter-master, who had been convicted in 1920 for having tried—during the Black Sea mutinies—to seize his ship and turn her over to the Soviets.

5. Romé, pp. 190–201.
6. Edwin Bickford Hooper, Dean C. Allard, and Oscar P. Fitzgerald, *The United States Navy and the Vietnam Conflict: The Setting of the Stage to 1959* (Washington, D.C.: Naval History Division, 1976), pp. 88–89.

4

COCHIN-CHINA (SAIGON)

WAITING FOR GODOT

In the colony of Cochin-China—where beautiful Saigon was the capital and where there were more French and assimilated Annamese than anywhere else in Indochina—they were now waiting for the other shoe to drop. The French were anxiously awaiting Leclerc, for their calvary to end. The nationalists were anxious for a deal. The communists were working to establish their control while there was time. For the rest, the great mass of the people were just watching to see how things were going to turn out before committing themselves to any side but their own.

Greater Saigon with a population even at this time of one million inhabitants is really two cities (see Map 4–1): Saigon proper and Cholon south across an arm of the Saigon (Dong-Nai) river. A major export-import, entrepôt, and shipping center, it is like several others here a double port. Cape Saint-Jacques—a roadstead at the mouth of the river, on the South China Sea—handles the larger deep-draft ships; and Saigon itself, fifty miles upriver, handles the rest. Tan-Son-Nhut airfield was just to its north. The city's principal exports were rice and rubber.

Map 4-1
MEKONG DELTA

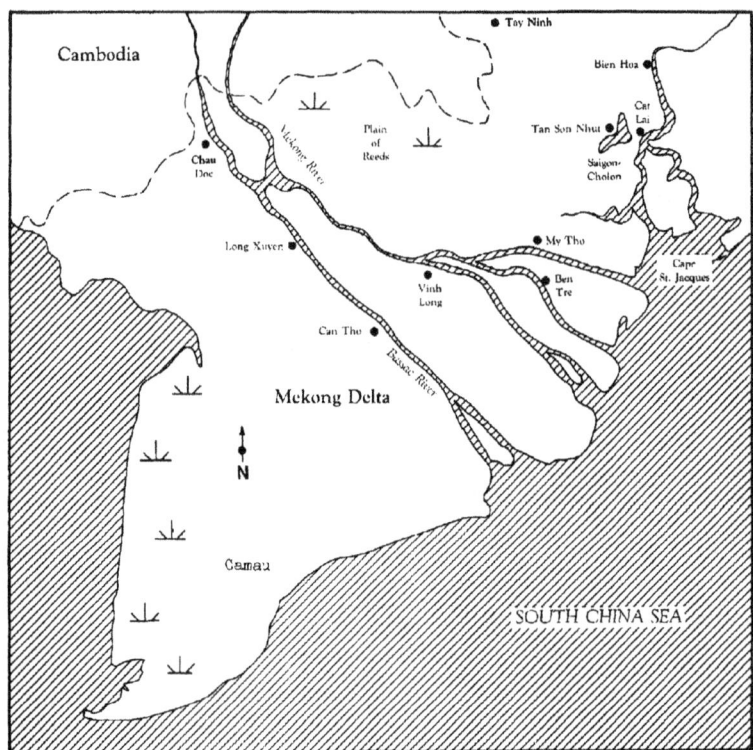

By plane and (increasingly) by ship, a dribble of fresh military and naval officers from the *métropole* had begun to surface in Indochina as early as August. Two naval lieutenants arrived in the Along Islands; one set up a small base at Port Wallut on the island of Ke-Bao at the northern end of the Fai-Tsi-Long chain, the other an outpost further south. A Gaullist intelligence (DGER) commander (de Riencourt) showed up in Saigon. He incidently did nothing for the Vichyites behind wire and accomplished little if anything else.

As we have seen, there already were several intelligence nets working in Indochina, operating out of Kunming (China) and Ceylon. In light of what was going on, one wonders who—if anyone—in Paris was reading their "take." Probably, Paris was too busy with other things closer to home for the take to attract much attention at the top.

COMAR TONKIN

One of the few among the *Marine*'s personnel to escape the Japanese coup was doughty Captain Andre Commentry, sometime chief of staff to Decoux and commander of *Lamotte-Picquet*, and now COMAR (NOIC) Tonkin, stationed in Hanoi. He brought out with him some 125 of his people, part of whom had to fight their way out. Two of his small armed launches—*Crayssac* and *Frézouls*—joined him.

Captain Commentry led his men north to the Gao-Tao and Fai-Tsi-Long Islands. More naval as well as army personnel drifted in, some via China. There they kept the tricolor flying, holding out—actively, under a variety of commands—until finally relieved a year later. Support—what there was of it—came from Pakhoi in South China. Commentry was himself called to Paris on July 17 to report and to receive new orders.

While Commentry was away, one of his lieutenants—Blanchard, by name—succeeded him. To Blanchard was confided the task of showing the tricolor off Haiphong on August 15, using *Crayssac* and *Frézouls*, the only remaining military craft. We pick up their story again later.[1]

The people Paris sent out at this point—Gaullists every one of them, it would seem—arrived in Indochina with a situational template that came straight out of their hard-won victory in Europe. Few had actually experienced France during the four-year occupation but carried with them an image of liberation clearly derived from Allied—especially Gaullist—propaganda. There were again here the cruel, hated *Milice* (read the Vichyite colonial old hands), with their foot on the throat of the brave *Maquis* (read Viet-Minh), and the Gaullist crusaders—themselves—come to restore freedom to the land. Unfortunately, the template did not coincide with Indochina reality.

The Viet-Minh's power base being in the north, here in the south they had to gain and keep control of the Nam-Bo. There was in the south, however, a considerable pro-French sentiment. Assimilation was well under way here. The French had, after all, been in the south for nearly a century. The Viets had to break this up any way they could.

THE FRANCO-BRITISH RETURN

Admiral Mountbatten had been ready to send troops to Indochina since August 19. It was not, however, until September 12— two days short of one month after the cease-fire—that elements of the Allied Control Commission arrived in Saigon. It was on that date that British Major General Douglas Gracey flew in, accompanied by a battalion of Gurkhas. He was to secure Saigon, then receive the enemy's formal surrender, disarm him, and send him home, meantime turning the country back to the French. Along with him came Royal Navy Captain Scott-Bell, designated temporary NOIC Saigon.

On September 12 also, Captain Commentry arrived in Saigon, via his own plane from Ceylon. In Paris on August 15 for debriefing and new orders, Commentry was on his way back two days later. He was to take over as provisional commander of the ships, units, and services of *Marine Indochine* as and when liberated, pending the arrival of a designated flag officer. Commentry was originally to pass by Kunming, waiting there until the situation further clarified itself. Stopping at Ceylon en route, he made his number with the French mission at Mountbatten's headquarters. They told him to head directly for Saigon, as Gracey would be there then. In Saigon, Commentry gathered together a staff, making Lieutenant Commander François Bramaud du Boucheron his chief of staff, and went to work.

Restoring Saigon's various naval activities to operational status presented Commentry with several serious obstacles:

- The Viet-Minh had made off with a good part of the *Marine*'s property.
- The French dispersal of their supplies before the March 9 *coup de force* meant locating and collecting it again.
- The Japanese recognized only British authority.
- The waters were full of mines, which he had no means to clear.

But the use of Saigon's facilities on a large scale would soon—too soon—become imperative. Major French and British reinforcements would begin arriving in about a month. Commentry had his work cut out for him.

The third key figure to arrive on the 12th was Army Lieutenant Colonel Rivier, Commentry's opposite. Rivier brought with him the first echelon of CEEO: a company of the 5th Colonial Infantry Regiment (RIC). Assisted by Navy technicians, Rivier took over control of the most basic public services—the power plant, the water works, and the Institut Pasteur—and got them going again.

Gracey's Allied Control Commission at that point had no intention of taking sides in Indochina's violent internal affairs. The Commission was to keep neutral, stay out of them, do its job, and leave. What could Gracey accomplish with one battalion of Gurkhas, in any case? His NOIC's small naval party—busy with minesweeping, control of shipping, and the port—was no better off.[2]

CEDILE

On the 24th of the previous month, a Gaullist calling himself delegate of the French Government in Cochin-China—Colonel/administrator of colonies/Commissioner Jean Cedile—had been parachuted in. With de Riencourt's help, Cedile made immediate contact with the Nam-Bo. He would talk with them. They would make a preliminary deal. Reason would prevail. Order would return. Reconstruction could begin.

Cedile appears as an ideologue. He had never served in Indochina. He ignored the advice of the local French and even of the pro-French Annamese. As a result he was quickly and thoroughly taken in by the Viets, who proceeded to use him for their own ends.

Cedile saw *les anciens* as the last traitors. They were to pay for their years of collaboration with Tokyo. Vichyites they were, who had not done their duty. He left them behind wire. Meanwhile, political prisoners whom he identified as victims of the "abhorred Decoux regime" he released from prison at once. The Annamese began to wonder what exactly was going on.

Saigon in those days was not to be believed. The city was in continuous turmoil. There were strikes and sabotage. There was no electricity, no water. There were continuous assassinations and kidnappings, in daylight, right on the streets. Rumors were rife, on every hand. The only authority the Viets recognized at all was that of the British. These they took care to stand clear of.

At this point, Colonel Cedile gave up. Cedile gave a press conference. Biting the bullet, he there announced publicly that he now saw that the Viets in no way represented popular opinion. Further, they were in no way capable of maintaining order. Order was the first priority, he said, after which a government could be formed. This *volte-face* took a lot of courage, but it was just a month too late, a month during which the French had irretrievably lost much local support.

What had happened also, however, was that the horror of what was going on drove the British right into the arms of the French. Neutrality was abandoned. Gracey could not get any of his work done as long as things continued as they were, in any case. He now stepped in and took a hand. In this, the British had had experience, too.

THE BATTLE FOR SAIGON

With Saigon steadily coming apart, between September 20 and 22, General Gracey initiated a series of measures designed to restore order. First, he decreed martial law. He limited the carrying of arms. He imposed a curfew and limited the right of assembly. Then he closed down those Annamese newspapers that were rabidly inciting revolt. Finally, he announced the death penalty for looters and saboteurs as well as assassins and set up military courts to enforce his orders.

Employing both his Indian and French forces, and in order to protect the central city, Gracey occupied the commissariat of police and the police stations. He seized Saigon's principal public buildings, including hospitals and the town hall, immediately turning the latter over to Cedile. The Japanese only looked on.

On the 23rd, the Viet-Minh reacted, fighting through the 24th and 25th to regain the central city. There was again no electricity, no water. Barricades appeared. Armed Viet-led mobs rampaged throughout the city. The market was burned. Communications were cut.

French men, women, and children who appeared in their path were tortured and killed with the utmost cruelty. The women were raped. But Gracey held on to the city. The Japanese were now forced to play their part.

Les anciens—needed now—were released September 20. They passed instantly from being probable Vichyite criminals to being combatants. But of the twelve-hundred-man naval group—beaten, starved, exhausted, sick—only some one-third remained fit to bear arms. From them was formed a provisional naval rifle battalion, under a Lieutenant Commander Picheral. The remainder of the military—the ground forces—scraped together sufficient men for two more battalions. Scarecrows dressed in rags and tatters, without even proper shoes, equipped with a wide miscellany of small arms and a few rounds of ammunition they were.

Most of the men had been in Indochina since at least 1940. In spite of everything, they had retained their military cohesion as POWs, and they showed it now. Their performance was worthy of the regulars they were, their gallantry superb. They were a welcome addition to the reconstituted 11th RIC.

On the night of the 25th came the climax. It was then that the Viet-led mobs took their final revenge. That night they attacked

Heraut City, a residential development occupied by both military and civilians and their families. Women, children, the aged—they were tortured wholesale, disembowled, killed, buried alive. When troops arrived, they found some 150 mutilated corpses. An estimated 200 people were kidnapped and never seen again. The lines were being drawn.[3]

The Viet-Minh were now run out of the city, laying siege to the city from the outside, reentering to loot and kill during the night. As more troops arrived, Greater Saigon was rapidly cleared, the Viets chased farther into the brush. Recovery of the south could begin.

From this point on, we are looking at de facto coalition warfare. Neither the British nor the French had sufficient troops in place to restore order even just in Saigon alone. To accomplish anything, they continually had to concert their actions, sometimes even pooling their forces. This relationship did not change until the French buildup finally freed the British to pull out. In Indochina, this worked well.

Once again, the Americans did nothing, paralysed by their own wartime propaganda. This was still the era of "Uncle Joe" Stalin and Mao Tse Tung, the agrarian reformer. Now those who paid any attention at all heard about "Uncle Ho" Chi Minh the nationalist, the struggling democrat.

More than two decades later, the imposition of martial law in Saigon on the 23rd was characterized by the authors of *The Pentagon Papers* as a *coup d'état*.[4] Unless murder and mob rule can be called government, there was then no *état* in Saigon to throw over. But the idea of there having been a *coup d'état* lived on. It helped paralyse us in 1945.

THE BUILDUP BEGINS

There now was obviously not going to be any peaceful turnover of authority from the Japanese to the British to the French. The Viets were seeing to that. A massive buildup of French and British forces had become a matter of urgency. Lead elements were already at sea.

For this reason, the next element to appear at Cape Saint-Jacques was the NOIC's naval party, which appeared on September 29. This included:

- a frigate
- nine minesweepers, to clear the channel up to Saigon
- four landing craft
- one oiler
- a depot ship
- a survey ship

The following day—the 30th—the frigate, three of the sweepers, and two LCIs—conned up by the NOIC himself—mounted the river and moored at Saigon. The NOIC and his party installed themselves in casern Francis Garnier and began work. There would be plenty to do.

Probably reacting to calls for help from General Gracey, the first large increment of French reinforcements debarked at Saigon on October 3. Mountbatten had placed two Dutch assault transports—*Queen Emma* and *Princess Beatrix*—at Leclerc's disposition, to move some of his available French, ready on Ceylon. They brought one thousand men of the 5th RIC and the 400-man Commando Ponchardier. A small, battered, old freighter—*Kontum*, an Indochina escapee—followed with seven hundred tons of cargo. Escorted by *Richelieu* and *Triomphant*, the urgent convoy left Trincomalee on September 27, arriving at Cape Saint-Jacques on the 3rd.

Richelieu drew too much water to go on all the way up to Saigon, so she stayed the fifty miles downriver at the Cape Saint-Jacques anchorage, unloading there. *Triomphant* and the two transports went right up to Saigon. There they received a tumultous welcome.

The 5th RIC, Commando Ponchardier, and landing parties

drawn from the ships' companies went ashore. *Richelieu*'s was a small battalion in size. Their first function was to prepare for and secure the reception of those others still on the way. The British—with the continued help of *les anciens*—held the town.

Les anciens began to be drawn on for all kinds of special duty. They became river and harbor pilots, naval advisors, and guides to a variety of newly arrived units. In Lower Cochin-China, one of them led a battalion of ethnic Cambodian partisans. There his word was law. It was, that is, until he became a political liability, when he was brought back in.

THE COMMENTRY–SCOTT-BELL AXIS

In the midst of a world turned upside down, NOIC Saigon (Captain Scott-Bell RN) and his two-hundred-man shore party had the following quite enormous responsibilities, for the satisfaction of which he was now directly responsible to a Commander-in-Chief British East Indies Station:

- To organize and direct the work of the port, using available French and IJN assets as needed
- To assure the security of all naval and merchant shipping, in cooperation with the 20th Indian Division
- To reestablish free access to the port from the sea, by river and canal
- To requisition whatever was needed for these tasks
- To assure—jointly with the 20th Indian Division—the surrender, disarming, and assembly for repatriation of all IJN forces

As can be seen, the responsibilities of Captains Commentry and Scott-Bell paralleled each other, with considerable actual overlap. Cooperation between them was close, the French contributing personnel and knowledge of the area. More and more, as the British relied on him, Commentry took over.

Minesweeping chores were shared between the Japanese and the British. Working together, they cleared the Cape Saint-Jacques anchorage, the channel up the river between it and Saigon, and the port itself. They had completed a rough sweep of the whole area before the arrival of the first large troop reinforcement convoys, although two transports managed to find stray mines of their own.

The NOIC also had a hydrographic survey ship working for him. She ran soundings in the Cape Saint-Jacques anchorage, in the river, and in the port, checking the charts. She ran a little behind, completing her work only on the 10th, but she got the most important soundings first. No damage was done.[5]

REINFORCEMENTS

Troops now began pouring in, the British first. Although some few of their advance party had been showing up in Saigon as early as October 2, British transports landed the principal elements of the 20th Indian Division, the first on the 6th, the last on the 16th. Nothing undue took place as some fifteen transports off-loaded their troops. The businesslike Indians immediately set about cleaning up Saigon's environs. They paid particular attention to the area around Tan-Son-Nhut field.

Beginning on the 15th, as they had become ready and on whatever ship had been at hand at the time, more French reinforcements pulled in. Thus came *Gloire, Suffren, Ville-de-Strasbourg, Quercy, Somali, Sénégalais, Gazelle, Annamite, Fantasque,* and last *Béarn,* on the 28th. *Béarn* had actually arrived at Cape Saint-Jacques on the 21st but had had to off-load part of her cargo before she could come up the river. AFN 2 was being bent about as far as it would go.[6]

The *Aéronavale*'s four available Catalina PBYs reached Saigon (Tan-Son-Nhut) between the 25th and the 30th. There they were joined by an ad hoc squadron composed of one Loire 130 and four small Aichi flying boats, helping take up the slack left by the four missing Catalina boats.

The attitude now of many of the returning French is well summed up in General Leclerc's statement at the airport on October 5th, made as he landed to assume command of his forces. "We have come," he said, "to reclaim our inheritance." For them, the Viet-Minh had pushed events past the point of no return. That was, after all, exactly what the Viets wanted to hear. Compromise would have cut the ground out from under them.

It was possible now to recognize two navies—the *Marine* "in white," the traditional blue water navy; and the one "in khaki," the estuarine and riverine navy, wearing work khakis all the time. For the estuarine (white water) and riverine (brown water) navy, the navy in white contributed transportation, big-gun fire support, landing parties, and a naval air arm. Offshore it patrolled, clamping down a blockade and isolating the arena. No large-scale operations on or from the sea would have been possible without it.

During the March 9 coup, the Japanese seized the remaining French merchant vessels still under the control of the Government General. Eleven of these had been destroyed or seriously damaged by Allied air attacks. That left five cargo vessels anchored in the Mekong theoretically capable of being put to work. Crews, however, had to be found to man them.

NOTES

1. Jean Gabrié, *Les Marines de la Guerre 1935–1945* (Vincennes: Service Historique de la Marine, 1994), pp. 48, 110; Henri Darrieus and Jean Quéguiner, *Historique de la Marine Française* (Novembre 1942–Août 1945), (Saint-Malo: Editions l'Ancre de Marine, 1994), p. 319.
2. Jacques Michel, ed., *La Marine Française en Indochine de 1939 à 1955* (Vincennes: Service Historique de la Marine, 1973), II (Août 1945–Decembre 1946), p. 98.
3. Ibid., pp. 98–100; Paul Romé, *Les Oubliés du Bout du Monde* (Paris: Editions Maritimes & d'Outre-Mer, 1983), pp. 195–211.
4. U.S. Department of Defense, *United States-Vietnam Relations: 1945–1967* (Washington, D.C.: GPO, 1971), passim.
5. Michel, pp. 100–2.
6. Ibid., pp. 102–3.

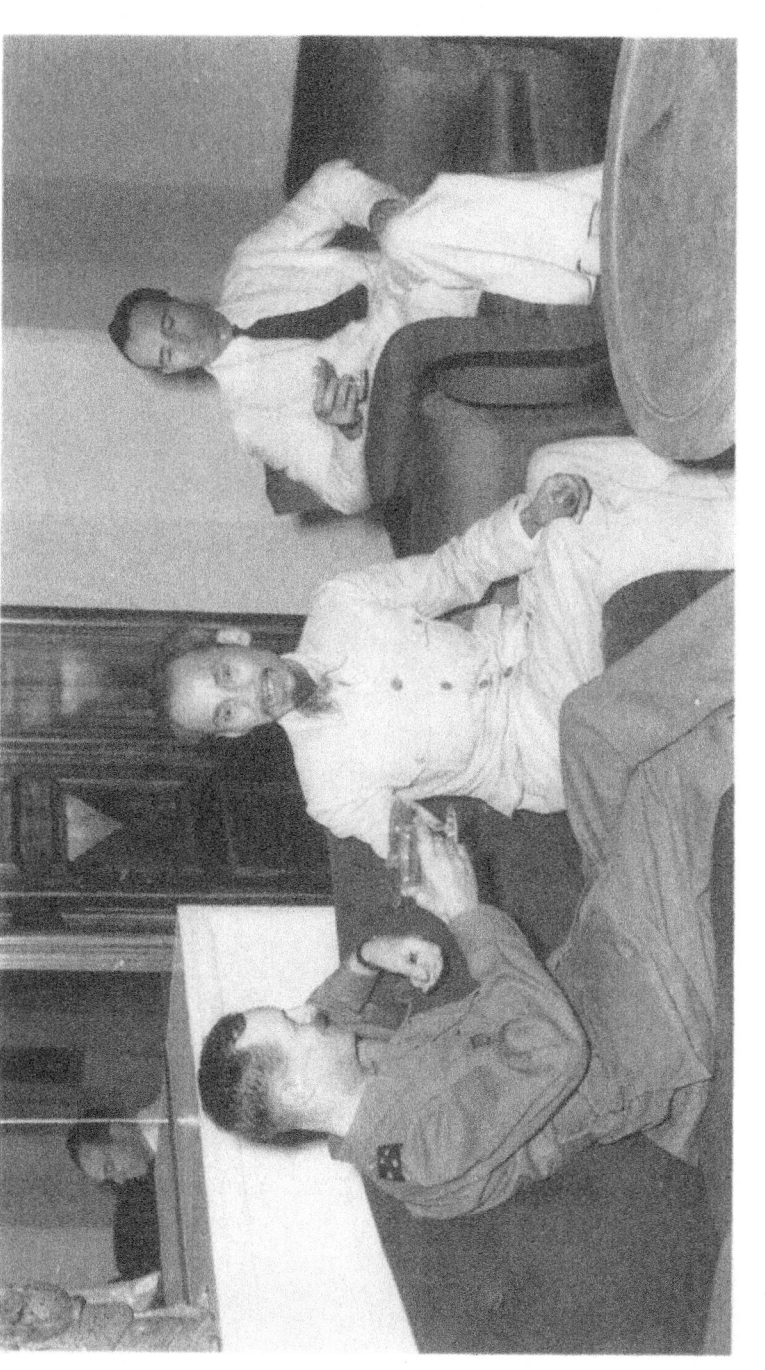

Leclerc, Ho Chi Minh, and Sainteny toast in Hanoi. For Ho, these talks bought time (to further organize, to eliminate rivals) and access to Paris (to propagandize communists there). (Courtesy SIRPA/ECPA, France)

Saigon river scene. (Courtesy SIRPA/ECPA, France)

Richelieu (fast battleship: Captain Merveilleux du Vignaux): 35,000 tons, eight 15-inch guns, 30 knots. In Indochina, her main battery was never fired. Returned home early, paid off. (Courtesy U.S. Naval Institute)

Gloire (light cruiser): 7,690 tons, nine 6-inch guns, 31 knots. *Montcalm* and *Georges-Leygues* were sisters. (Courtesy U.S. Naval Institute)

Emile-Bertin (light cruiser/minelayer): 5,886 tons, nine 6-inch guns, 34 knots. Far East squadron flagship. (Courtesy U.S. Naval Institute)

Triomphant (destroyer leader): 2,569 tons, five 5-inch guns, 37 knots. *Fantasque* was sister. Rated by the French as light cruiser. (Courtesy U.S. Naval Institute)

Algérien (ex–U.S. destroyer escort): 1,240 tons, three 3-inch guns, 21 knots. *Sénégalais* and *Somali* were sisters. (Courtesy U.S. Naval Institute)

Annamite (sloop): 640 tons, one 90-millimeter gun, 20 knots. *Gazelle* was sister. (Courtesy SIRPA/ECPA, France)

British LCI 166 (Sub-lieutenant Davidson RN). (Courtesy SIRPA/ECPA, France)

French ex-U.S. LCI. (Courtesy U.S. Naval Institute)

Fusiliers-Marins disembarking in Saigon. (Courtesy SIRPA/ECPA, France)

U.S.-built LCT. (Courtesy U.S. Naval Institute)

U.S. LCVP. Behind and to the left is a spoon-bowed U.S. LCA. (Courtesy U.S. Naval Institute)

French river assault group, led by a gunboat. (Courtesy U.S. Naval Institute)

U.S.-built French *Catalina* patrol bomber (PBY): amphibious, 200 knots, 3,000 miles, machine guns/bombs/torpedoes/depth charges/mines. (Courtesy SIRPA/ECPA, France)

Loire 130 flying boat: 140 knots, 510 miles, machine guns/bombs. Designed for shipboard use. (Courtesy U.S. Naval Institute)

LSTs beached, discharging troops. (Courtesy U.S. Naval Institute)

River craft approaching Ninh-Binh. (Courtesy U.S. Naval Institute)

U.S.-built motor minesweeper (YMS): 215 tons (136 feet), one 3-inch gun, sweep gear, 12 knots. Used by both the United States and France in and off Haiphong. (Courtesy U.S. Naval Institute)

5

THE MEKONG DELTA AND SOUTH ANNAM

EXPANDING CONTROL

While General Gracey's 20th Indian Division secured what amounted to a lodgment, the French spent several days marrying up troops and equipment just ashore and in having a good think. Gracey then assumed responsibility for pushing out to the north of Saigon and for keeping open the routes to the sea (Cape Saint-Jacques) and the airport. Leclerc assumed responsibility for pacification of the area to the south and west.

Leclerc disposed at this time of about forty-five hundred men, including one company from BMEO, Commando Ponchardier, and landing parties from *Richelieu*, *Suffren*, and *Gloire*. He was closely supported by sloops *Annamite* and *Gazelle*.

Delta terrain is complex: a network of twisted creeks, dikes, and canals; dense jungle and hot, humid swamps; and everywhere rice fields. Scattered about are islandlike villages edged with mangrove, palm, bamboo, and banana. During the monsoon rains (summer, in the south) the delta floods, and the only practicable means of transport is by water.

In this delta, the *Marine* watched while Leclerc's armor relearned a lesson hard-won in Holland in the fall of 1944. In such country, the effort of a whole corps can narrow down to that of a single rifle squad slogging down a muddy road or fording a stream, bypassing a blown bridge. Movements are rapidly channeled, roads cratered. Bridges are easily blown, and there are lots of them. Something more was obviously called for.

Thus, geography (the nature of the delta), the enemy (river-dependent), and the task in hand (pacification) all combined to make a riverine force indispensable. Indochina's waterways were the only real avenues of penetration into the country's interior. They would be used.

FIRST STEPS

Commander François Jaubert led BMEO until Captain Robert Kilian arrived to assume command. Charged with organizing a riverine force, Jaubert unhesitatingly requisitioned anything river-worthy. He sent officers scrounging for suitable river craft, motors, weapons, and spare parts. Headquarters was set up in the former Saigon Yacht Club, with a statue of Buddha in the main hall, invoking the protection of the local god.

Early on, in the fighting just outside of Saigon, a lieutenant (Paul Romé) from the provisional naval battalion found a treasure—a group of four rusty, abandoned flat-bottomed motorized river barges. Several had lost their motors, but parts were found to make one usable enough to demonstrate with. No one was ever sure if the old Bolinder motor would start, and if so in which direction—ahead or back—it would go. The barges lacked beauty, but they did the job.

These barges had formerly belonged to a firm called Gressier, hauling some two hundred tons of rice each, at four knots, up from the fields of the Bassac to the mills of Cholon. Using these Gressier barges—as refitted—the lieutenant began ferrying troops across and along nearby waterways. The idea quickly caught on.[1]

As built, these barges offered no protection from either the weather or the enemy to the crew, passengers, or cargo. A small wheelhouse, armor, and weapons were gradually added. Smaller, faster, more agile craft came along as escorts or scouts, whenever they were in and available for such duty. Assault units came to be built around them.

SOUTH AND WEST (OPERATION MOUSSAC)

BMEO had soon scraped together what it called a Naval Infantry River Flotilla. This flotilla's immediate task was to reestablish a permanent French presence along the lower Mekong and the Bassac. This was done at once. The next objectives were three strategically located provincial capitals: My-Tho, Vinh-Long, Can-Tho, all held by the Viet-Minh. They were towns of around sixty thousand people strung northeast to southwest across the throat of delta traffic.

The first to be taken was the nearest—My-Tho, situated at the juncture of several highways, on the north bank of the main shipping channel to Phnom Penh. My-Tho had originally been assigned to a combined column of Army and Navy units moving out overland from Saigon. However, Leclerc's column found the road cratered and the bridges blown. Going through the paddies, in the mud, across streams was grindingly slow, if possible at all.

Thus, contrary to original plans, it was BMEO that on October 25 reoccupied My-Tho. Commando Ponchardier (Lieutenant, later Lieutenant Commander Pierre Ponchardier)—armed with Brens and Stens—came in by water on a pickup collection of small river craft supported and supplied by the sloops *Gazelle* and *Annamite* and two British LCIs, surprising the rebels at 0200. By the time the overland column reached My-Tho, it had been in the hands of the commando for forty-eight hours. The staffs had another think.

That same week, in a similar joint operation, another contingent of the brigade carried by *Annamite* took control of Vinh-Long and held it. The drill for this was getting set: land by surprise, rush up the main (usually the only) street with squads peeling off left and right as they went, seize the key (symbolic, more solid) buildings (the administrator's residence, the church, the power station, the bank, the hospital, and the former gendarmerie casern), clean up. But by now the rebels were alerted. Success came harder.

Then on the 30th, a ninety-man force from Ponchardier's commando took Can-Tho. At Can-Tho, the Japanese provided the exception to their usual behavior. There the Viets had killed an officer and several men of the small Japanese garrison. The Japanese colonel felt that he could not go home without avenging these losses and cooperated wholeheartedly with Ponchardier's "Tigers," to the point of actively joining in on the cleanup.

The surrounding country was now alive with swarms of rebels, buzzing around like annoyed bees. The commandos—really only light infantry—could not remain passive and live. Many times outnumbered, they attacked so as not to be attacked. Using newly occupied Can-Tho only as a base, the force patrolled aggressively, ran ambushes, and raided, to keep the Viets off balance. This they did.

EXPANSION

BMEO (Commander Jaubert then Captain Kilian) soon absorbed the provisional naval battalion into its ranks. It took over the operation of the original four Gressier barges, soon adding whatever landing craft it could get its hands on. The French bought a number from the Singapore British; the Saigon British left them others. Some were somehow even bought in Manila. *Fusilier* units were permanently assigned, to give them either an organic assault party or a cadre for something larger, in addition to the crew.

BMEO could then go anywhere in the area. For short distances, the barges were each capable of carrying an entire rifle company. They were thus capable of landing troops to attack a strong point; hit a flank; block or close off given areas; even, within limits, seize, occupy, and hold ground.

BMEO also carried out a number of auxiliary chores. Its barges brought up food, water, fuel, ammunition, and engineer supplies. It evacuated casualties. It housed unit command posts until command could be shifted ashore. After its barges were armed, they provided an integral source of close fire support and were given names taken from those of the armored barges France employed in the Crimean War—*Lave, Devastation, Tonnante, Foudre.*

At first, My-Tho, Vinh-Long, and Can-Tho, though secure, remained isolated outposts in rebel-controlled country. A large ex-Japanese two-hundred-ton motorized junk turned over by the British was manned by the *Fusiliers* and named *Arcachonnaise*. Armed, she successfully took over the logistic support of these towns. From these towns, Leclerc pushed outwards, until order was restored to the whole delta.

In early December, ubiquitous transport *Béarn* delivered fourteen landing craft, assault (LCA) and six landing craft, vehicle and personnel (LCVP), purchased from the British at Singapore, the first of many such. These landing craft were gradually armed and armored and given the names of the "petites amies" of the petty officers in charge, names like *Doudou, Ramatou, Vahine, Sampanière* and *Marinière.*

In January and February a Gressier barge and two LCAs helped pacify the delta's southwest areas, in spite of having to clear numerous Viet barricades defended by fire. Another such force cleared the way for troops pushing towards Cape Camau. By the end of February, almost all of Cochin-China was freed.[2]

As the area of French control widened and outlying villages were cleared, the *Fusiliers* regularly seized Viet arms, ammunition, and papers. Some of the weapons were kept by the *Fusiliers* for their own use. Some weapons were turned over to volunteer Indo-Chinese *Tirailleur* units, for subsequent village defense. The rest were burned or blown up. One of the remaining notables was designated (or confirmed) village chief. The market was opened. The *Fusiliers* then had to move on.

Arcachonnaise was joined by sisters *Lorientaise* and *Paimpolaise*. All three gradually acquired a considerable support capability, each being armed with a seventy-five-millimeter gun, a twenty-millimeter automatic gun, and several machine guns. They remained constrained by their relatively deep draft, but they had capacious holds.

BMEO REORGANIZES AND EXPANDS FURTHER

BMEO was fast losing its structure as a regimental combat team. To the already assimilated *anciens* of the provisional naval battalion were added the men from the various landing parties constantly being left behind when their ships returned home. A new de facto structure was emerging, a consolidated one, better suited to the many miniamphibious and other waterway-related operations in which it was more and more engaged.

By January 1946, BMEO had reached a strength of some three thousand officers and men. It now counted about fifty landing craft and perhaps thirty assorted junks, sampans, launches, and scows. Somewhat more discrete organization was demanded, so a second river flotilla was soon formed. It would be earmarked for the north, when the time came.

After being established, river flotillas did not operate as entire units. They fielded assault units, mini-task forces tailored to the specific task in hand. These became known as *divisions d'infanterie navale d'assaut*, or *dinassauts*. For the military historian, they marked this era.

A typical river flotilla assault unit at this point could include the following major elements, with all of the craft manned by *Fusilier* boatcrews:

- 2 Gressier barges (armored and armed)
- 2 LCAs
- 2 LCVPs
- 1 ex-IJN landing craft
- 1 tug and two lighters
- 2 *Fusilier* squads (organic assault parties or armed guards)

Cooperating with this unit could be perhaps a *Fusilier* rifle company, or even a whole battalion, embarked and ashore.

BMEO did much more, however, than man the river flotillas, important as they were. Among other things, it took over responsibility for Captain Commentry's old unit in Along Bay, now using Hongay and Port-Wallut as bases from which to police the pirate-infested bay, the mainland coast, and the islands. It furnished armed guards and escorts for merchant convoys traveling coastal and inland waters. It patrolled these waterways. BMEO itself retained an organic infantry battalion, in addition to everything else.[3]

Relations with the British were very cordial. The British indicated that they wanted to retain control of Saigon's commercial port until their troop convoys—already en route—had arrived and were off-loaded. It was so agreed. A French naval officer was assigned to Phnom-Penh as liaison officer to the British there; another went to Camranh for the same purpose.

BMEO set up its principal base at Phu-My—near Saigon—with quarters, offices, warehouses, and workshops with slips. It set up stations at My-Tho and Can-Tho. Nothing was very grand, making use of abandoned or half-destroyed buildings and the like—but it did the job.

THE LANDING PARTIES

On October 22, *Richelieu*'s landing party (Millet)—supported by *Gazelle*—launched an operation to occupy Gocong, some thirty miles to Saigon's south. Landing at night at Bac du Vaico, it was met by a hail of fire. Nonetheless, Gocong was occupied on the 28th. *Richelieu*'s party then cleared the surrounding area, holding Gocong until mid-December when the party was relieved by a battalion of the 23rd RIC. Gocong had cost one officer and five men.

Suffren's landing party (Magnien) came ashore at Saigon on October 26. It remained in and around Saigon, patrolling, backing up the police, and guarding warehouses and offices.

Gloire's landing party (Guitard) arrived ashore at the end of October. Its duties paralleled those of *Suffren*'s men.

Emile-Bertin only arrived in Saigon November 21. Its party came ashore on December 5. It helped push out the controlled area around Saigon: at Nha-Be to the south, after landing behind rebel lines; at Rach-Cat to the north; at Buc-Hoa to the southwest, where two of its men fell into rebel hands and were executed; at Cat-Lai to the northwest.

Cooperation with the Army was not always as easy as it should have been, especially with elements unused to working with the river flotillas, for the higher commands were invariably in army hands. Staff discussions could get quite heated because, for instance, army officers did not allow for the fact that in tidal areas the twice daily tides put unconditional constraints on operational timetables. In the delta, these tides were felt as far as two hundred miles inland. Unless landing craft kept strictly to these tables, they could easily be trapped on one side of a bar or another, or even be left high and dry.

This tended to reinforce BMEO's already strong inclination to the permanent marriage of specific *Fusilier* units with one flotilla or another. Some flexibility was admittedly thereby surrendered, but performance in this increasingly specialized warfare was as a result more rapid and much more expert, and the casualties were lower.

Another problem jointness produced was that after an isolated objective was taken, the Army tended to soak up BMEO's amphibious assets on purely logistic tasks. Carried too far, this cut into the brigade's offensive capabilities. Only in the offense was all its potential used. Navy spokesmen on senior staff were called for here. Added they soon were.

TERROR AS A WEAPON

The Viet-Minh had begun to use terror everywhere as a weapon right from the beginning—from before the French returned—and they continued to do so. This reinforced the Viet threat of action against the noncooperative. None of this encouraged the angry *Fusiliers* to saintliness, thus helping alienate them from the *nha-qué*.

Viet propaganda made the most of the French response, ignoring the fact that they—the Viets—sometimes deliberately caused it.

When the *Fusiliers* took Gocong, they were met at the entrance by the bodies of two hundred Viet prisoners, beheaded by the Viets and tied to stakes. At one point, of ninety-six parish priests in the Catholic diocese of Saigon, seven were known to have been killed, five had been taken hostage, and there was no news of fifty-two others. At least two pro-French political leaders in Saigon were buried alive. No quarter was being asked, and none was given.

During the course of one of the early operations in the delta, BMEO came across the remains of one of their first convoys, missing since November 18. The circumstances of the loss—as they were exposed—were a shock, the news of which passed like wildfire through the brigade.

On the 18th, a tug towing several civilian junks, with an armed guard of some twenty men, en route from My-Tho to Saigon, vanished into thin air. It was never heard from again.

It was discovered that the missing convoy had been trapped in a narrow creek and completely shot up. The lucky ones died immediately. The survivors were paraded by the Viets through nearby villages and publicly humiliated, then tortured. In each of the villages one of the *Fusiliers* was killed, his body atrociously mutilated and thrown into the jungle. Only a harbinger of things to come, this was.[4]

A very few pacifiers in the midst of a sea of frightfulness, Ponchardier's commandos went to war as if to war. In December, in "the Ponch's" area near Can-Tho, the Viets in an ambush seized a French soldier. They decapitated him and hung his head on the Bassac bank along with a sign saying, "This is what we do to the French."

The "Tigers" thereupon went out and caught a half dozen Viets. The next morning at dawn, on the same bank, six Viet heads were neatly lined up, along with a banner reading, "Here is what we do to Viets who try to terrorise us." That finished that particular matter.

NORTH—NHA-TRANG

It had been much the same to the north of Saigon, considering the radical differences of terrain. Here was no lush delta, all flat, but a fertile narrow coastal plain varying from twelve to fifty miles in width, backed by sizable wooded hills. Distances in Annam were greater, too. Unlike in the deltas, the coast here was rocky.

Annamese towns consisted for the most part of clusters of thatched houses, villages grouped together inside walls and moats, defended by a relatively large citadel looming over all. The Viets tended to seize the citadels, dominating the countryside from there. But the progress of pacification here too depended on lines of communication resting on the sea. The *Marine* therefore played its usual key role here, too. Nha-Trang offers one example.

Triomphant (Jubelin) departed Saigon on October 15, escorting a British LCI, headed north. The LCI was carrying supplies destined for the approximately thirteen hundred French civilians barricaded in Nha-Trang, three hundred miles up the coast. *Triomphant* was to secure the delivery of what was primarily food.

The Franco-British force arrived off Nha-Trang on the 17th, at which time *Triomphant* landed a detachment of sixty men. The Viet-Minh protested the presence of *Triomphant* as well as the landing party and demanded their recall.

Commander Jubelin refused the Viet ultimatum and requested orders. While Saigon blew hot and cold, the Viets attacked the civilian perimeter on the 22nd, killing one woman. *Richelieu* was called in on the 24th, restoring order. In all this, the twelve-hundred-man Japanese garrison was only a very reluctant ally.

The British LCI successfully landed her food. *Richelieu* was recalled on the 29th. *Triomphant* was relieved by *Fantasque* on November 6; a destroyer type was kept on station off Nha-Trang from then on.

By mid-November, additional French forces—a battalion of the 6th RIC—arrived, and Nha-Trang was secure. The 6th RIC was able now to bring the backcountry under control, covered by navy guns.

Nevertheless, the Viets continued to dominate the roads leading into Nha-Trang from the south, and maintenance of the French position there depended entirely on supplies brought in by sea. It was to be three months before the Army fought its way up Route Coloniale No. 1 and cleared the way into town.[5]

THE BUILDUP CONTINUES

In the midst of everything, the French buildup continued as fast as could be done. This included key commanders and their staffs. *Emile-Bertin*, as we have seen, arrived in Saigon on November 21. Flagship, she brought Admiral Auboyneau. Admiral Graziani—on-scene since October 27—had taken over as COMAR Indochina two days later, relieving Captain Commentry, who moved to Leclerc's staff.

All naval participation in Leclerc's operations was henceforward coordinated by a Bureau Marine, headed up by Commentry. At this point, this meant the sloops, the landing parties, elements of the river flotilla, and naval aircraft.

Aéronavale's patrol planes were kept busy. They flew reconnaissance missions. They delivered key personnel and critical supplies. They flew medical evacuation runs. They dropped thousands of psychological warfare (psywar) fliers. And they endlessly patrolled coastal waters.

The cruisers *Tourville* and *Duquesne* now enter the scene. *Tourville* departed Toulon December 5 for Saigon with 610 passengers and fifty tons of matériel. *Duquesne* departed for Saigon on the 22nd with 420 passengers—the last elements of BMEO—and various priority goods.

Richelieu departed for France on December 29, leaving behind at Leclerc's request her landing party. A hammer used to swat flies, she was never to return. She was replaced by the two newly arrived cruisers and by two colonial gunboats (sloops).

Normal rotation had begun, too. *Suffren* departed Saigon on October 27, leaving behind at Leclerc's request her landing party, but taking back home five hundred men, including four hundred hospital cases.

By early December, French military personnel—still concentrated in Cochin-China—had swelled to some 21,500. Saigon was militarily secure, the Viet-Minh driven back underground, into the Annamese quarter or out into the bush.

After a formal visit to Saigon by Admiral Mountbatten, who first satisfied himself as to the situation, he and d'Argenlieu agreed on the gradual withdrawal of the now twenty thousand British troops. Details coordinated between their staffs, the British drawdown began immediately. On December 26 the British NOIC left, leaving in Saigon only a liaison team. Leclerc now had the entire "con."

THE JAPANESE

The approximately seventy thousand Japanese personnel found south of the 16th parallel at the close of the war were originally to be disarmed, concentrated, and repatriated as soon as possible, by and under the authority of an Allied Control Commission. Shipping was to be provided initially by the Allied pool, later by the Japanese themselves.

General Gracey headed up this commission in addition to his other duties as commander of all Allied land forces south of the 16th parallel.

With Gracey's Franco-British forces fully occupied on their vital military roles, the Allied Control Commission had atrophied and so in November was dissolved as such. The French took over the entire operation, and the British went on to other things.

A combination of circumstances had delayed repatriation of the Japanese. The victors' assets were for several months soaked up in general pacification efforts. For longer than originally thought, the Japanese turned out to be necessary to help keep order, and some they did. With local labor in such a chaotic state, and workshops scarce, the Japanese were also found useful in keeping local support functions going. More cooperative than the Army, IJN assets were especially useful to the RN, which would have had serious difficulty operating without them. Their disarmament was delayed until late-November.

But anyway by mid-December 1945, most Japanese Army personnel in the south had been concentrated at Cape Saint-Jacques, Navy personnel at Camp Thu-Dau-Mot. The last twenty thousand were expected to arrive at Cape Saint-Jacques by the 20th—one problem less for Leclerc.

INTERVAL

With the effective military pacification of the south, the first of the two phases of the expedition to recover Indochina was complete. The French now had a base for the second phase, the occupation of the north. There was, however, an interval of time in which the French built themselves further up and prepared the military and political ground for what had to come next. Meanwhile, life continued.

Operation Gaur (January 23–29, 1946, for the *Marine*) was launched to consolidate the pacification of South Annam. Gaur being executed essentially by land forces, the *Marine* participated by providing various ships for gunfire support or to execute tactical or strategic feints.

Gaur's concept of operations called for two motorized columns— one from the north (Ban-Me-Thuot), the other from the south (Saigon)—to clear a way to Nha-Trang. As they approached, troops at Nha-Trang were to break out and seize the troublesome inland citadel of Khan-Hoa.

The Marine's contribution to Gaur was to be as follows:

- *Emile-Bertin* was to demonstrate to the north, cutting rebel communications and harassing them.
- The usual destroyer type was to remain on station at Nha-Trang.
- *Tourville*, a destroyer and two minesweepers were to fake an amphibious landing at Camranh.
- *Sénégalais* and *Somali* were to demonstrate far to the south.

Everything having gone essentially as planned, on completion of their roles, the participating ships remained up north a few days as insurance then returned to Saigon to prepare for the relief of Tonkin. From February 15, not one ship from Gaur remained off South Annam.[6]

CLEANING UP

The French Army and Navy subsequently conducted another successful series of minor operations further north along the Central Annam coast, supported from the sea and along the rivers. By the close of the first quarter of 1946, all of the major population centers and lines of communication in Cochin-China and Annam south of the 16th parallel were in French hands. In a major sense, this was thanks to the *Marine*.

Nonetheless, pacification here remained somehow unreal. The *Marine* could go where it wanted. The rebels were strong only on land and only in some places. Taking advantage of the opportunity, for instance, a French officer went ashore on the island of Tagne at the entrance to Camranh Bay. Tagne was the site of a still-embryo naval station, still garrisoned by Japanese troops. This officer confirmed the Japanese commander's orders—to resist any attack by the rebels and to maintain intact all installations, matériel, and weapons until relief. Without interference, that done, the French officer then returned to his ship. All this while the mainland was alive with rebels. Indochina had become a beautiful, deadly never-never land.

Still cleaning up, attention was now turned to reoccupation of the Phu-Quoc Islands in the Gulf of Siam, and of Poulo-Condore, off Cape Saint-Jacques. Sloop *Gracieuse* and an LST were involved. Both objectives were taken without resistance. With the *Marine* uncontested master of the sea, the Viets had no choice.

SAIGON

Life in these days in Saigon was unreal, a mélange of overexcited lives, luxury, courage, and death. Continual heat and humidity aggravated the nervous tension. But life—even family life—went on. Commerce was restored. Traffic moved freely. Cafés and restaurants did a booming business. One shopped at Ben-Thanh market or met friends on the Hotel Continental's terrace or in its lobby. The strain was relieved at the Cercle Sportif or in the gambling houses of Cholon.

The Cercle Sportif was a major French meeting place. It boasted a swimming pool, tennis courts, a good library, a restaurant and a bar. All Saigon's movers and shakers sooner or later showed up at the bar. There the latest news and gossip—military, political, economic, social—could be picked up, long before it appeared anywhere else.

At evening, one strolled down the beautiful Rue Catinat to the Quai d'Argonne with one's wife. One remarked only casually that the gunfire or explosion one heard was "over near the market" or "towards Cholon" and went on doing whatever one was doing at the time.

HOPE?

Behind all this, the frightfulness went on. Collaborating Annamites were sentenced to death by rump communist courts and not infrequently simply buried alive. The horror had no limits. One day, as a French couple came out of Phu-My botanical gardens, they were shot down by Viet terrorists. Their bodies were then doused with gasoline and burned, a warning for all the passersby to see.

Another day, two bodies floated past the quays, down the Saigon River. One was that of a tall blond man, the other that of a small dark-haired Annamite girl. They were face to face, spit on the same bamboo.[7]

But increasingly, there was no way out. Any drawdown of French troops risked, in effect, sowing doubt among those Annamites who remained loyal to the French cause. These pro-French would be subject to ferocious reprisals as soon as the French were too weak to protect them. They had already seen what those reprisals were like. The tragedy was that as long as the north remained a steady source of infection—arms, money, men, and ideas—there could be no idea that the terror would stop. The situation had to change. It was about to. Preparations were under way. The bar at the Cercle was full of it.

NOTES

1. Paul Romé, *Les Oubliés du Bout du Monde* (Paris: Editions Maritimes & d'Outre-Mer, 1983), pp. 224–29; Jean-Pierre Bernier, *Le Commando des Tigres*, Jacques Grancher, ed. (Paris: Maulde et Renou, 1995), passim; Yannick Guiberteau, *La Dévastation* (Paris: Albin Michel, 1984), passim.

2. Jacques Michel, ed., *La Marine Française en Indochine de 1939 à 1955* (Vincennes: Service Historique de la Marine, 1973), II (Août 1945–Decembre 1946), pp. 295–97, 299–302.

3. Ibid., p. 328.

4. Ibid., pp. 105, 118–20, 129; Robert Kilian, *History and Memories: The Naval Infantrymen in Indochina* (Paris: Editions Berger-Levrault, 1948), passim.

5. Bernard Favin-Lévêque, *Souvenirs de Mer et d'Ailleurs* (Versailles: Editions des 7 Vents, 1990), pp. 123–25.

6. Michel, pp. 144–45.

7. Georges Debat, *Marine Oblige* (Paris: Flammarion, 1974), pp. 277–79.

6

TONKIN

THE STAGE—THE NORTH

From here begins almost another whole story, that of the second phase of the expedition to recover Indochina for France: the takeover in Tonkin, including negotiations with the Nationalist Chinese and the Viet-Minh. There were the initial efforts to integrate the Viet-Minh into the French Union. Finally came the amphibious occupation of Haiphong, followed by the move into Hanoi and the rest of the north.

Up here in the north, the French would be alone. There would be no Britain to take up any slack while the French gathered their forces. For d'Argenlieu and Leclerc, here would be the final test; for Auboyneau, too.

Above the 16th parallel, the situation facing the French was more difficult than it was in the south, even, insofar as the French were concerned, at least. Here there were three potentially hostile players—the Nationalist Chinese as well as the Japanese and, above all, the Viet-Minh.

The north is Tonkin, the Red River Delta. Through it run three major rivers—the Red, the Black, and the Clear (see Map 6–1).

The first two both originate in Southern China, but it is the Red that is the principal waterway. Like the southern delta, Tonkin is normally rice-rich, although less so. It is the most densely populated region of Vietnam.

The Tonkin Delta is flat, but contains only a few highways (*routes coloniales*) or other roads and fewer rail lines. Both use numerous bridges and are easily cut. In contrast, the waterways are many and have many branches; because of this, they are difficult to police.

The northeast monsoon brings with it intense fogs, rough seas, and pounding surf. Against the latter two, shelter can be had. During the monsoon rains (winter, in the north), the delta floods here too.

Tonkin, with two-thirds of the Annamese people, includes the neighbor cities of Hanoi (230,000 people), the capital, and Haiphong (140,000 people), the port. These are the industrial heart of Indochina. There are rich deposits of coal and metal ores in the hills. Thirty thousand French lived up there.

Haiphong exported vast quantities of rice to China. The city also served as an outlet to the sea for the Southern Chinese province of Yunan and was connected by rail. In spite of its difficult approaches, Haiphong was a busy, colorful China Sea port.

THE PLAYERS

The Chinese were for the moment the principal players. Their huge mass had pressed down on the Indo-Chinese peninsula for centuries. They had no love for the French, who had taken Tonkin from them only half a century earlier. When Chunking, in 1945, heard that the French had managed to maintain a toehold in the far northeast—in the Along islands—it tried to force the French out but failed.

Chiang Kai-shek's Nationalist (Kuomintang or Chunking) Chinese moved with peace into the northern half of Indochina as the Allied representative for the disarmament of the Japanese and their repatriation—this, pending further decisions on the future of the area. Chiang may himself actually have had territorial designs in

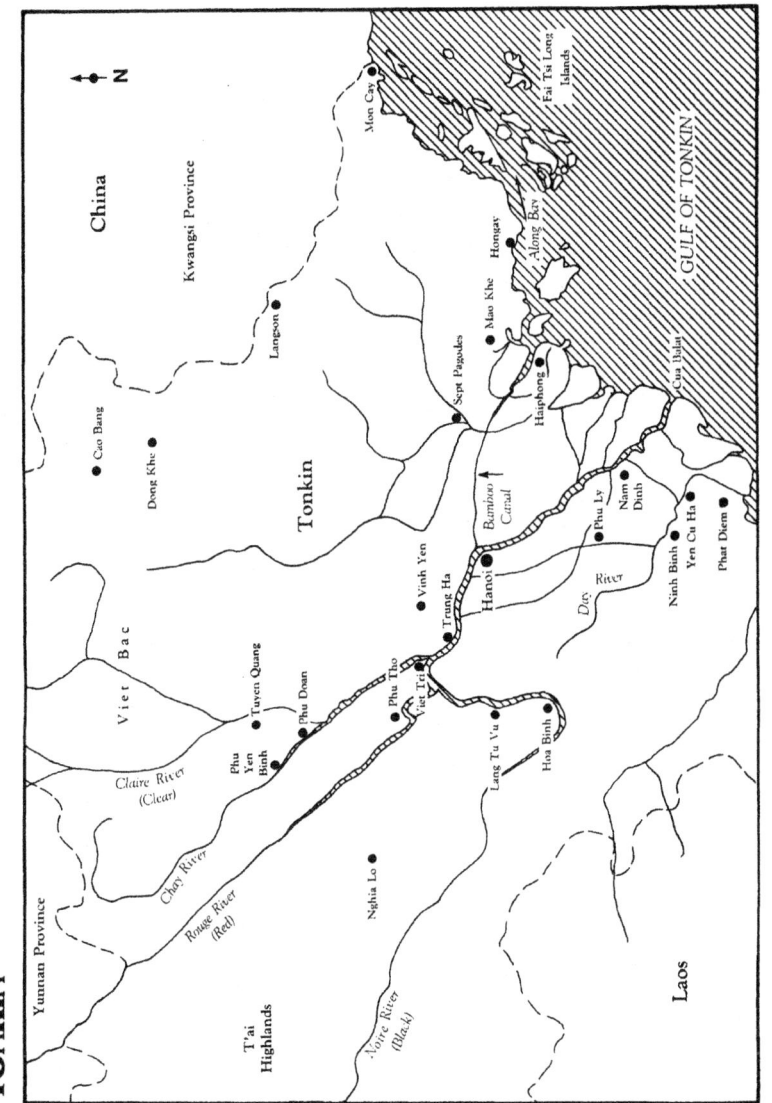

Map 6–1
TONKIN

the north, which had centuries-old ties to China. In any case, he did not particularly welcome the return of any European power on his southern border.

Chiang sent in his First Army Group, commanded by a General Lu-Han. This army group (we would call it an army) had 180,000 men organized into four armies (we would call them corps). They plundered the north, looting the area of everything valuable they could move. They manipulated the Vietnamese currency so as to develop enormous profits, too. Gradually Chiang's options withered away, and he began to maneuver for terms.

The attitudes and actions of the Japanese in the north paralleled those of the south. In the beginning, they fomented the maximum of trouble, then they tried to keep out of the way until they could get home. As long as they were armed, they were supposed to help maintain order but only did so under duress.

The Viet-Minh were something else again. Back in August, Viet columns—numbering hardly more than ten thousand badly armed men—taking advantage of Allied confusion had occupied most of Tonkin, starting with Hanoi and including Haiphong and the delta. There Ho Chi Minh assumed governmental power as President of the Vietnamese Democratic Republic. There the Chinese, Japanese, and even the United States all gave him limited support.

There were also two other political parties active in the north. Up here there were the VNQDD—nationalist, the Dai-Viet was strong in the Haiphong area—and the Dong-Minh-Hoi—pro-Chinese, paid political tools. The latter were available to Lu-Han should Ho Chi Minh become too much of an embarrassment and have to be replaced. They helped keep the Viets in line.

EARLY DAYS

As has been mentioned, the French in August 1945 had several intelligence units active from Kunming (Yunan), just to the north. The DGER mission was headed by Commandant (Major) Jean Sainteny, a pre-war planter with some knowledge of the scene. Sainteny was to play a large role in the north throughout this period, eventually being named Commissioner for Tonkin.

Sainteny maneuvered his way into Hanoi on the 22nd, a hitchhiker on a U.S. plane. In Hanoi Sainteny found a most confusing political free-for-all, with Ho Chi Minh gaining the upper hand. Although at first Sainteny had no official status there, he did much to ease the tense relations between the resident French and the Viet-Minh. D'Argenlieu responded by naming him commissioner, and Sainteny remained in Hanoi.

Leclerc himself saw Hanoi as the last step in his task in Indochina. He saw the danger in a prolonged Chinese stay in the north, and it worried him. He saw also that the failure to reach a political settlement with Ho could drive Ho into the brush again, with the possibility of a prolonged guerrilla war ahead of him.

For several months right after the Japanese surrender, then, Paris was represented in the north only by a commissioner heading a small politico-military mission in Hanoi, by a navy lieutenant and a launch in Haiphong, by the military and naval fragments active in Along Bay, and by *les anciens* still behind wire in Hanoi and Haiphong. It was a shame.

But the situation was somewhat better in fact than it looked. Commissioner Sainteny developed very good personal rapport with President Ho. The French made a very useful counterweight to the Chinese for Ho—for the moment.

The last French POWs held by the Japanese in the north were only released on October 5. Those held by the Viets had already been released on September 16, probably reflecting Sainteny's good relations with Ho.[1] They remained, however, essentially unarmed, held in the Citadel.

Hanoi began tentatively to return to life. One walked the Rue Paul-Bert, took tea at the Hotel Metropole, visited the cafés. The Viets maintained a tenuous kind of order, for the moment. Air traffic with the south opened up.

ALONG BAY

Even in the earliest days after the Japanese March *coup*, there was never a time when the tricolor was not flying somewhere in Along Bay. We have already mentioned Captain Commentry. In those days he hid out in the bays, swamps, and creeks of Northern Tonkin and Southern China, using a base at Port Wallut. The Captain's navy at one time included armed launches *Frézouls* (Blanchard) and *Crayssac* (Vilar), naval escapees such as armed junks *Audacieuse* and *Vieux-Charles*. Various local prizes were taken over and used for patrol, also.

The initial effort to reestablish the French position in the north was made by those two launches. On August 11 they were in Hongay, at the bottom of Along Bay. On the 15th they arrived off Haiphong. On the 16th Lieutenant Blanchard determinedly led the two craft into Haiphong and tied up. They accomplished little, being kept in semiarrest until they left. *Crayssac* was later seized by the Viets while carrying out a medical evacuation at Hongay.

Special attention was paid all along to Along Bay. It boasted extensive, exceptionally fine anchorages and a good harbor—Hongay. Coal mines at nearby Campha were important to the Indo-Chinese economy. The lower end of the bay—twenty miles east of Haiphong and seventy miles southwest of the Chinese border—was a natural base for further operations as Leclerc came north. This he was going to do.

In mid-November the arrival of the first of a series of French destroyers (ex-U.S. DEs)—*Sénégalais*, then *Somali, Algérien*—allowed the French to consolidate their position there. *Sénégalais* apparently arrived just in time to cut up a Viet assault on one of the islands the French already held.

Piracy being endemic up here, restoration of order now was the main task. Inadequately policed during the troubles—sometimes with political cover—the pirates were out of control. BMEO took over the task, in addition to its other duties. Because these pirates were full-time fishermen and pirates only of opportunity, a wide *Fusilier* presence usually did the job.[2]

THE U.S. ROLE

During the whole of this period, the United States played several separate but interrelated roles in Indochina. A U.S. military mission had arrived in Hanoi on August 18, 1945. This mission was dissolved April 1, 1946, but a portion reemerged in Saigon as technical attachés to our consulate there.

At this point, the U.S. Seventh Fleet (Vice Admiral Thomas C. Kinkaid) had assumed operational responsibility for the waters around northern Indochina. Its Commander, Amphibious Force provided the ships for initial redeployment of Chinese troops and repatriation of the Japanese (this task was later picked up by Chinese and Japanese civilian shipping). The USN manned a liaison office in Haiphong until completion of this task.

The United States was a shadowy background figure in those early days, too. The OSS had representatives both with *Crayssac*'s Lieutenant Vilar when he was seized (Vilar was never seen again) and with the Viets, to whom we had furnished some arms. Basically, we were trying to find out what was going on. Then in September the OSS had disappeared from view.

Ho Chi Minh may at one point have had some idea that he could involve Washington in some sort of trusteeship, on the order of the Philippines. It was mentioned in several places. But in retrospect this was almost certainly only a ploy intended to gain Ho additional support against Paris. Independence was what Ho really was after. In any event the idea was not picked up, disappearing into the silence of the files.

During May 1946 a group of ten U.S. naval officers and petty officers arrived in Saigon. These officers—mostly engineers—had assisted with the fitting out of our landing craft the French had purchased in Manila, and then accompanied them over. They then disappear from view.

DIPLOMATIC PRELIMINARIES—CHINA

Before the French could return to the north—especially as compared to what had been involved in the south—extensive diplomatic preparations had to be made. Four-way negotiations were opened at Chunking, involving China, France, Britain, and the United States, covering the relief of Lu-Han's army group by Leclerc's men. The Hanoi government was not consulted in this, at any point.

As a result, on February 28, 1946, the French ambassador to China and the Chinese foreign minister signed several interconnected accords. In them Paris made a number of concessions concerning Chunking's use of Haiphong and the Red River for trade purposes. Lu-Han was to be gone by the end of March, brought out by U.S. ships. But it was the French who paid for these accords.

It is in a sense only a minor historic irony, but just as Haiphong and the Red River helped in 1940 to precipitate Indochina's wartime crisis, so in 1946 they were to help end it. In the February 28 accords, the French were to reserve in the port of Haiphong a special zone, including warehouses and, if possible, the quays necessary for the free transit of merchandise originating in or destined for China. Customs supervision of that zone was to be Chinese.

Rail cars on the Indochina-Yunan railroad transiting between Haiphong's special zone and China were to be sealed by said customs.

Cabotage and internal navigation—along the coasts, up and down the rivers, and in the ports—was to be governed by the principle of the most favored nation, but the terms would not be less favorable than those enjoyed by the locals on both sides. Free goods were to remain free on these craft, too, of course.[3]

Chiang Kai-shek had allowed Ho Chi Minh to continue to govern in Hanoi because the Chinese had moved in purely as a matter of convenience. Chiang had to have considered Ho as one of his very minor puppets, which in some sense he had been. Against Chiang, Ho could only lose, so he kept out of Chiang's way. Smiling, Ho battened down the hatches to wait things out.

It is probable that events elsewhere in China—the communists were taking over the north—expedited these accords. Lu-Han's 180,000 men were more needed there in the north than waiting out an increasingly stale hand in Tonkin, as they were.

TONKIN 77

DIPLOMATIC PRELIMINARIES—HANOI

The Chunking accords of February 28 took care of Paris's external preparations for returning north. By themselves, they did nothing for the just-as-mandatory internal accords. These boded to be even more difficult than the first. But in the long run, for various differing reasons, it suited both Saigon and Hanoi that there be politico-military arrangements, so there were.

There had therefore been parallel negotiations under way in tense Hanoi between Commissioner Sainteny—acting for d'Argenlieu as High Commissioner—and Ho Chi Minh concerning the future status of Indochina. Sainteny succeeded in hammering out an agreement of sorts with Ho only the same day (March 6) the returning French were to steam up Haiphong's Cua-Cam.

The Saigon-Hanoi accord of March 6 was preliminary and provisional, but it did accept relief of the Chinese by the French, and it did recognize a self-governing (not independent) Republic of Vietnam as part of an Indo-Chinese federation within the French Union. The French military—after having relieved the Chinese—were to be drawn down over a period of five years, until the French were to hold only selected naval and air bases, along with the means to defend them.[4]

D'Argenlieu through Sainteny had succeeded in compromising the impossible. An Annamese nationalist rebel calling himself president working towards a dictatorship of the proletariat had agreed to accept self-governing colonial status. A French nationalist viceroy representing a democracy had agreed to accept him on these terms. D'Argenlieu apparently meant all this. Ho could not have.

Not settled then, however, was the future of Cochin-China. This southernmost of the three Kys had a somewhat different history and ethnic makeup than the north. The south was effectively pacified and was recovering from the wounds of war. It had returned more or less to a kind of normalcy. It owed nothing to the north. Significant numbers of local Annamese leaders willing to work with the French could be found here. The Nam-Bo was still there, certainly, but underground now.

In fact, the creation of a separate Cochin-Chinese state independent of the north was being bruted. A provisional government for the south was already in place. A plebiscite was mentioned by some. Ho wanted the Chinese out, however, and he was willing to let that one wait.

SUCCESS

Franco-Vietnamese cooperation seemed to be going very well. As of March 7, theoretically, there was peace in Indochina, on the surface, at least. The basic accord of the 6th was followed by an annex dated the following day. A complementary military accord was completed April 3, the last missing piece.

The agreement on military cooperation—unlike the other two—was signed between French General Salan and Viet General Giap. This last accord detailed the stationing of French and Viet troops throughout the north. It also created a mixed central commission of liaison and control seated at Hanoi, to settle the minor frictions that would inevitably arise.[5]

On March 8, in a separate Franco-British arrangement, the French formally agreed to take over Mountbatten's remaining Indochina duties. Faced with this development, the CCS on March 28 formally designated the French as the Allied agent for repatriating the Japanese. The British thereby ceased to have any responsibility in this area at all. Withdrawal of the last vestiges of a British presence—of the last of the British forces—was completed by April.

Relief of the Chinese troops by the French was more or less completed by around March 31, although there were still minor clashes between them. But the actual Chinese evacuation continued to be delayed. For one thing, the opium harvest was due in and that might have held things up. Finally, on September 18 the last twenty-eight hundred men departed from Haiphong on U.S. ships, as agreed.

That was Indochina as seen in the chancelleries and far-off capitals. Now it all had to be made real. Operation Bentré was designed to do just that. Preparations had been under way for some time. The expedition's end was in sight.

COMMAND AND STAFF

For Bentré, Leclerc took personal overall military command. Genesuper's chief of staff was a Colonel Guillebon, as operations officer a Colonel Lecomte, as intelligence officer a Colonel Repiton-Préneuf. The senior staff was thus ground forces–heavy. Something else was needed. But a commander under pressure, in a hurry, needs to have his own staff. He did—his Bureau Marine, whose function was to ensure all required coordination between Leclerc and the various participating naval authorities.

This bureau was directed by—who else?—Captain Commentry. With a full head of silver hair, Commentry in these days was known to his staff as "Le Vieux Charles," or (not in front of him) "Blanche-Neige." Collaboration was both efficient and effective.[6]

Armed with tide tables and ships' drafts, the Bureau Marine worked closely with Genesuper's Operations (3rd) Section, the one charged with the preparation and running of Bentré. Whenever Commentry's people invoked whatever purely naval constraint on something, Lecomte understood and went along with it. This was not always the case with his brothers in arms.

The Bureau Marine also worked with Genesuper's 4th Staff Section—Supply and Logistics—to prepare the force's loading plans. Getting the right people, equipment, and supplies on board the right ships and craft at the right time in the face of continually shifting command, intelligence, and technical requirements was a problem that was not finally settled until the last ship had left. And then it was to change again.

But Bentré had to work! The French liaison mission to Singapore at almost the last minute obtained from the British two LSTs, eight LCIs, eight LCMs, and twenty-five LCAs. Du Boucheron, assisted by pickup staffs and crews, took delivery and brought them up to Saigon.

The small Indochina freighter *Kontum* appears again now, loaded with a cargo of rice and sent up north. After innumerable difficulties with the Chinese, her cargo was split between the occupiers and Campha's coal miners. *Kontum* returned to Saigon loaded to her marks with two thousand tons of precious coal—and information, too.⁷

NOTES

1. Georges Thierry d'Argenlieu, *Chronique d'Indochine 1945–1947* (Paris: Editions Albin Michel, 1985), pp. 97–98.
2. Jacques Michel, ed., *La Marine Française en Indochine de 1939 à 1955* (Vincennes: Service Historique de la Marine, 1973), II (Août 1945–Decembre 1946), pp. 307–10.
3. Ibid., pp. 37–50; Bernard Favin-Lévêque, *Souvenirs de Mer et d'Ailleurs* (Versailles: Editions des 7 Vents, 1990), pp. 134–35.
4. D'Argenlieu, pp. 173–93; Michel, pp. 53–67; Lévêque, pp. 134–35.
5. D'Argenlieu, pp. 179–93.
6. Lévêque, pp. 130, 132.
7. Michel, p. 114.

7

BENTRÉ

MISSION

Operation Bentré's mission was—in its broadest terms, simply put—just to reoccupy the Tonkin (Red River) Delta. Geography translated this plain statement into a major two-phase campaign. Originally, D'Argenlieu's (Leclerc's) general concept of operations to relieve the Chinese and to move in alongside the Viet-Minh troops was as described here.

Bentré's first phase was to be the simultaneous amphibious bringing in of French troops to the Tonkinese ports of Haiphong and Hongay, both efforts to take place at 080600 March local. Every precaution was to be taken that the operation came across as a normal administrative relief of the Chinese, respecting as well the guarantees made to the Ho regime. From there, having relieved the Chinese forces in those port cities, and using those cities as a base, Bentré was to march on Hanoi. A pause here was anticipated, to marry up equipment and troops.

In a second phase, a column from the 2nd Armored Division, reinforced by infantry from the 9th DIC and supported by a ghost from the past—the *Fusiliers*' armored regiment—would be pushed from Haiphong the hundred miles (150 kilometers) inland to Hanoi along Route Coloniale No. 5, relieving the Chinese and holding it.

Operation Bentré was the most important amphibious operation the *Marine* had up to then mounted by its own means. It was the culmination of its work in Indochina.

In both cities, the Tonkinese population had been aroused to a fever pitch by Viet agitation. In both cities, the security of the resident French—there were approximately twenty thousand of them in Hanoi alone—was essentially in the hands of a disarmed weak French garrison released by the Japanese only in October. It was necessary not to further arouse the locals.[1] Not until there was no choice, in any case.

Bentré got underway for Tonkin from Saigon and Camranh Bay, most sailing on or about March 1. Time was once again a critical factor. Tides were a serious limiting factor, as always in these waters. And no one knew for sure what kind of reception the troops would actually get anyway. French leadership was indeed once again going to be tested.

ORGANIZATION

Army units involved in this operation included the following:

- The 9th Colonial Infantry Division, made up of three infantry regiments, four artillery battalions, two engineer battalions, and one reconnaissance squadron
- A mobile group from the 2nd Armored Division
- BMEO (attached)
- Support units

These Army units totaled some 20,700 men. They were commanded by a General Valluy.

The following special units also had to be counted in the tally:

- A large ad hoc regiment made up of troops returned from China
- The special operations units working around Along Bay
- The Hanoi garrison (forty-five hundred men), with twenty-five hundred more in Haiphong
- Commando Ponchardier

Navy units involved in this operation were formed into Force Z and included the following:

- Cruisers *Emile-Bertin* (flag), *Tourville*, and *Duquesne*
- Destroyer-leaders *Triomphant* and *Fantasque*
- Destroyer *Algérien*
- Sloops *Gazelle, Chevreuil,* and *Savorgnan-de-Brazza*
- Transports *Béarn* and *Barfleur* and six merchantmen
- A minesweeper division (four)
- Two LSTs and about forty assorted landing craft

Most of the major naval units, it will be noted, were remnants of the old pre–World War II French Navy. Some had even been laid up in 1944. Bentré offered them one last hurrah.

Force Z was commanded by Admiral Auboyneau himself. All of FNEO was to participate, with the exception of *Somali* (on a major mission to Manila), *Annamite* (on an operation in the south), and one sweeper. *La Grandière* was assigned but not yet joined. Force Z represented a maximum effort, and was assembled at Saigon, Cape Saint-Jacques, Camranh, and other southern ports in anticipation of orders.

Six merchantmen for use as transports had been located, chartered, loaded, and assembled at Camranh, also awaiting orders. These were: *Céphée, Bételgeuse, Camille-Porcher, Saint-Loubert-Bie, Espérance,* and *Eridan*. Some had had difficulty loading. They were all slow, some very slow. Two would run aground during the operation's crisis.

Kontum—the small freighter—had apparently been working up in the Along archipelago. She is listed as part of the fleet train, a contingency asset. So was *Chevreuil*.

In place already in the north were an acting COMAR Tonkin installed in the citadel at Hanoi, complete with radio. There was also a clandestine local post under the orders of a COMAR Haiphong, also with radio.

The following Navy units also had to be counted in the tally:

- The special operations units working around Along Bay
- Three Catalina PBYs based in the Along Islands and three Aichi flying boats carried on *Béarn*
- The sixty-man Haiphong naval detachment, reinforced for Bentré with forty more officers and men

Air Force units involved in this operation included the following:

- Eighteen Spitfire fighters, used as fighter-bombers
- Twenty Dakota C-47 cargo planes
- A scattering of Junkers Ju-52 transports

These were based initially at Saigon, but anticipated displacing to Haiphong after its field was open.[2]

OTHER FORCES

There were three other potentially dangerous armed forces with which d'Argenlieu had to be prepared to deal. There were the Chinese, in effective control of Tonkin's larger population centers. Lu-Han's army group (we would call it an army) was made up of the 60th Army, garrisoning Haiphong and the lower delta, and the 90th Army, based in Hanoi. Hanoi itself held twelve thousand of his troops, Haiphong twenty thousand, Hongay two thousand, and

Doson ten thousand waiting to be loaded out. They were supposed to be in the north to keep order until relieved by the French; they kept to the cities and towns and were apt to defer to the Viet-Minh outside them.

The disarming and evacuation of the Japanese had not by any means been completed. There were some thirty thousand of them assembled in cantonments in the vicinity of the following towns and cities: Hanoi, thirty-five hundred; Haiphong, fifteen hundred; Quang-Yen, fifteen thousand; elsewhere, ten thousand. They too had previously given the Viets support, and the one thousand Japanese liaison officers spread throughout Tonkin constituted a good means of contact. Even the Chinese had found Japanese technicians of use.

Last but certainly not least, there were the Viet-Minh rebels. In the north, their numbers were growing, having approximately doubled to 20,000 in a year. Hanoi held 2,500, Haiphong 5,000, Hongay a token 100, Doson 150. Not all were armed; those that were carried an assortment of French, Japanese, and U.S.-parachuted weapons.

French diplomacy had theoretically just finished neutralizing these three potentially dangerous armed forces, one way or the other. The Chunking agreements of February 28 and the Saigon-Hanoi accord of March 6 were milestone events, clearing the way for Bentré. In any case, of the three, only Lu-Han really threatened the success of d'Argenlieu's effort. He was the one to watch.

THE OBJECTIVE PORT

The port of Haiphong is actually located some twenty miles from the China sea, on a river called the Cua-Cam (see Map 7–1). It is inaccessible to any vessels of more than six meters draft. The Cam is even more shallow at its entrance, so to reach the port of Haiphong from the sea, ships first mounted the parallel, deeper Cua-Nam-Trieu. When vessels reached the Vu-Yen cut— a dredged channel across the mud flat that separated the two riv-

Map 7-1
HAIPHONG AND APPROACHES

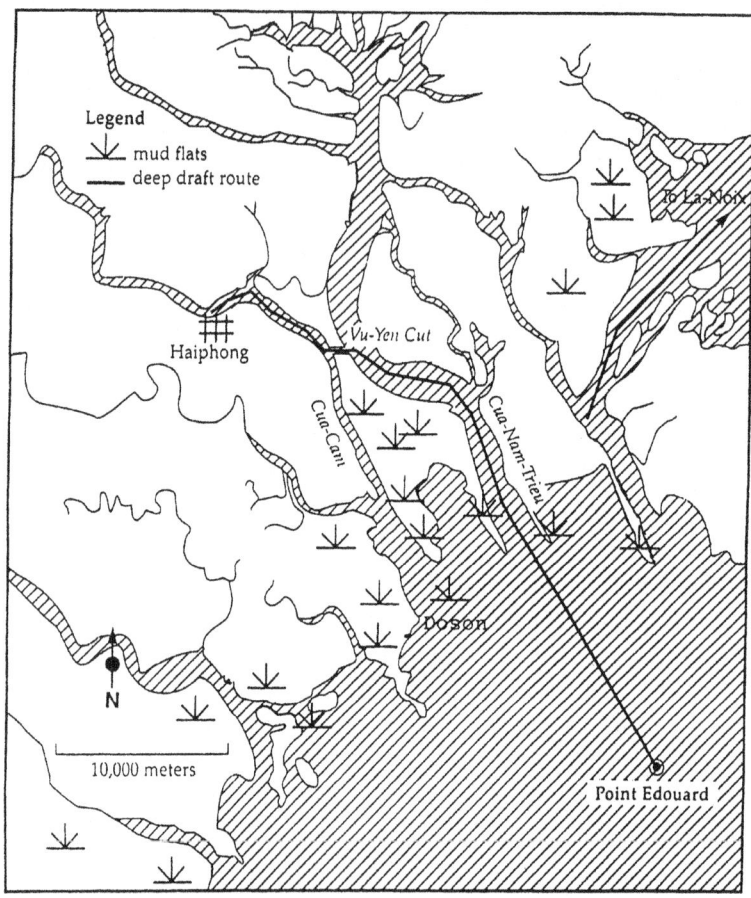

ers—they moved over to the Cam. Ships then continued on to the port. The cut was not usable at night or in fog; or when improperly dredged.

To get the largest ships possible up into Haiphong, the French had to enter the Nam-Trieu—which had a bar of its own—during the slack of a good monsoon-swollen high spring tide. Even then, only the *Marine*'s destroyer-leaders would make it inside. This was what drove the push for a landing on March 6.

Haiphong, however, is tied by a thirty-mile series of waterways to a sheltered anchorage usable by larger ships. There at a place called La-Noix these ships could off-load in all weathers into barges and their cargoes lightered to port. There were no plans to use La-Noix.

There were a couple of outports handy. Hongay, for one, was essentially a small coal port located on the northeastern edge of the delta, near Campha's mines. From it, Hanoi was one hundred miles distant to the southwest. La-Noix anchorage was nearby, conveniently connected to Hongay. But there were three gaps on the Hanoi road that had to be crossed by ferry. Even smaller Doson was essentially a peninsula some twenty miles to Haiphong's southeast, with good hard road access and good beaches. These two could supplement but not really replace Haiphong, limited as it was.[3]

COASTAL DEFENSES

The approach to Haiphong was defended not only by geography, but also by a number of man-made improvements. The French had built some before the war. These the Chinese had taken over. The United States had added to these during its wartime operations in the area. Any of these could slow down the landing, even defeat it.

The approach to Haiphong was protected by both coastal artillery and mines. There were two strong coastal batteries at Appowan, only one of which appeared still active. The approach was also protected by both magnetic and acoustic mines, which U.S. aircraft laid during the war. There were also U.S. submarine-laid fields in among the offshore islands.

The French had already requested our assistance in clearing the mines, at the highest formal level. For political reasons, however, this request had been shunted aside. But it is a long way from Washington to the fleet. Some sweeping went on, in spite of it all.

It was just operations-connected, and Washington only heard of it after the fact.

During the war, Haiphong's navigational lights and buoys had been destroyed. By war's end, two cargo ships had been sunk in and were blocking the main deep-draft channel. By the end of November these too were reported clear. Ships of all kinds had been moving in these waters for months now, but about mines one could never be sure.

U.S. MINESWEEPING

Earlier Washington positions being whatever they might have then been, U.S. ships had tasks in those waters. There were Japanese to be repatriated and Chinese to be redeployed. There were also mines there, but there were sweepers available. The key here was the Nationalist Chinese. U.S. forces had orders to support Chinese occupation of strategic positions in the Chinese theater. Admiral Kinkaid's Seventh Fleet was first to move the Chinese 52nd and 62nd Armies from Haiphong to Manchuria, using U.S. Navy assets. At one point the United States had three Navy liaison officers assigned to Haiphong. But first, these waters had to be cleared.

One American minesweeping division (four YMS 136-foot sweepers) was assigned to the area. Japanese forces in Haiphong already had two seventy-foot wooden-hulled trawlers available for such work.

By October 1945, IJN sweepers had begun operations in the Haiphong River. The four USN sweepers meantime swept offshore Haiphong and the sea lanes off the Norways. When finished there, these sweepers plus additional LCVPs joined the IJN to finish their job.

Both the 52nd and the 62nd Chinese Armies were evacuated from the Haiphong area by the end of December. The USN left for other business. It had cleared channels through the Haiphong approaches and up into Haiphong itself. Also usable now were the beaches at Doson. These had been sufficient for our particular purposes.

FORCE Z

While all this was going on, the French were busy in the south planning their return north. Though the return would be military in concept, the result was going to have to be political, showing the watching Annamese that the French could again dominate the north, that they could again govern. Bentré had to succeed the first time. Leclerc's staff put a maximum effort into it.

The *Marine*'s assigned role in Bentré was a conventional one, set out as follows:

- To transport the initial participating Army units (personnel and matériel) to the landing area
- To land these units as close to Haiphong's airfield (Cat-Bi) as they could, and in the port of Haiphong, if possible; if not, to land these units at alternative Hongay and Doson; and to continue to support them once ashore
- To secure the maritime and riverine lines of communication and to supervise navigation on them
- To continue in this role as long as necessary, bringing in later reinforcements and supplies
- To execute a diversion on the Annamese coast en route, to mislead the rebels as to Bentré's actual objective

To accomplish all this, Force Z—the *Marine*'s contribution to Bentré—was created.

CONCEPT OF OPERATIONS

Bentré's concept of maneuver was governed by the following special constraints:

- There were 20,000 French civilians in Hanoi, 1,200 in Haiphong, and 250 in Hongay.
- To avoid difficulties with the Chinese, it would not be

possible to take Haiphong by surprise, nor to lay down preparatory fire.

- Collusion between subordinate Chinese units and the rebels was probable, and there was the possibility that the rebels even alone would resist any reoccupation of the north.
- There were strong coastal artillery defenses and mines.

As finally worked out, the operational concept included the following key elements:

- Force Z would not approach within view of the shore at Haiphong before nightfall on the eve of the chosen day.
- Landing craft would be off-loaded from their ships and assault groups assembled at an offshore anchorage during the night.
- Naval gunfire would be available at once, against the coastal batteries, if need be.
- Ships and craft would complete their aproach to land while it was still dark, arriving at the Vu-Yen cut at dawn.
- The Vu-Yen cut would be seized at once and held.
- Haiphong airfield and the ports of Haiphong and Hongay would be seized as a matter of priority.
- Control of the waterways linking Haiphong with Along Bay would be established as a matter of priority.
- Plans for the major landing were made alternatively for the outports of Hongay and Doson alone, should that be needed.
- A diversion would be carried out at Quinhon to mislead the rebels.[4]

UNDERWAY

Bentré now had to be moved the eight hundred miles (fourteen hundred kilometers) from Saigon north to Haiphong. The accords with China had been signed on February 28th. An agreement with Hanoi seemed near. By the 28th, troops and equipment were essentially loaded. If a landing at Haiphong on March 6th—the last day for two weeks on which tides would be high enough to do so—was to be made, it was time to start. Orders were issued. Between Saigon and the anchorage off Haiphong, Force Z was broken down into three simple essentially administrative groupings. These divisions were based on forming convoys of ships having the same basic vessel sailing characteristics, seaworthiness, and speed:

- **Convoy no. 1**: transports and cargo ships (military and civilian) escorted by the colonial gunboat *Savorgnan-de-Brazza*
- **Convoy no. 2**: minesweepers, LSTs, and LCIs (either slow and/or very tender to sea and wind) escorted by the sloop *Gazelle* and the destroyer *Algérien*
- **Cruiser force**: three cruisers and two destroyer-leaders acting as a covering force, ready to provide gunfire support on call (to carry out diversion en route)[5]

Bentré's leading elements got underway for Haiphong the following day—March 1, 1946. Only at Saigon and Cape Saint-Jacques could the large ships and heavy equipment have been loaded out, and only Haiphong was a feasible port of entry for a force of that size. Camranh Bay was still only a protected anchorage, useful for assembly of convoys, and so it was used.

BIR HACHEIM

On the hypothesis that he must be prepared to use all his force, if there was no other choice, was he ever to return to the north, Leclerc also readied an outrageous gamble—a concurrent subsidiary airborne assault on Hanoi (Operation Bir-Hacheim). His plan was to free and rearm the forty-five hundred *anciens* disarmed by the Japanese and held there in the citadel by the Viets. Perhaps one thousand of these troops were still combat-worthy. For this operation, Leclerc planned to use Pierre Ponchardier's naval commando, parachuting them in on the day. It was a risky idea, but it might work, creating a diversion if nothing else.

The basic concept of Bir Hacheim was, once on the ground, for the commando to bring in sufficient weapons to rearm *les anciens*, Leclerc then adding them to his slim force. Several of Ponchardier's officers had been sent in ahead to locate specific objectives, prepare and mark the necessary drop zones, and arrange their defense. They were to ready sabotage of Hanoi's communications system. And they were to be ready to seize Ho and other Viet leaders, to paralyze countermoves by the rebels. A tall order, that.

The main problem was, Hanoi's citadel, Bach-Mai airstrip and radio, and the government were all on the north side of the Red River. Gia-Lam airfield was on the south, and it would be needed for the extra weapons. Two drop zones were chosen: one in the rice fields south of the river, from which to seize the airfield; the other directly on the river's sand banks, to seize Doumer Bridge, which crossed it.

Ponchardier and his men were ready now any time. If indeed anyone could pull this off, the "Ponch" could. But one 400-man commando (read only a light rifle battalion) to take on Hanoi? Much would depend on how quickly Leclerc linked up his two forces.

NOTES

1. Georges Thierry d'Argenlieu, *Chronique d'Indochine 1945–1947* (Paris: Editions Albin Michel, 1985), pp. 178–79; Bernard Favin-Lévêque, *Souvenirs de Mer et d'Ailleurs* (Versailles: Editions des 7 Vents, 1990), pp. 131–33.

2. Jacques Michel, ed., *La Marine Française en Indochine de 1939 à 1955* (Vincennes: Service Historique de la Marine, 1973), II (Août 1945–Decembre 1946), pp. 151–52.

3. Edwin Bickford Hooper, Dean C. Allard, and Oscar P. Fitzgerald, *The United States Navy and the Vietnam Conflict: The Setting of the Stage to*

1959 (Washington, D.C.: Naval History Division, 1976), pp. 108–9; Lévêque, p. 132; Michel, pp. 154–56.
 4. Michel, p. 157.
 5. Ibid., p. 165.

8

THE LANDING

THE LAST ACT

On the evening of March 5, Force Z assembled off Haiphong, duly anchored at point Edouard—the best of several preplanned options—sorted itself out, and prepared to present itself the following morning at the cut, exactly as planned. But then things began to go wrong, and the French command was really tested.

Winter in the delta was ending, and with it the monsoon. The weather was still moderate, the waterways high. There is mention of high tides, of March 6 being the last day suitable for a landing for the next two weeks, but with every delay now the constraints on a landing—hydrographic, political, military—would loom larger, almost no matter what.

With every day, above all, the Viet-Minh became more entrenched. They organized and recruited, and they eliminated their enemies.

For the French, in any case, Bentré represented a maximum politico-military effort. Such an effort could not be maintained for an indefinite period. The whole thing would lose its edge. Cooped up in barracks or on board ship, the troops would grow stale.

CURTAIN

After having made landfall off the Norways, Force Z's various convoys headed for preplanned point Edouard, located three miles south of the entrance to the Cua-Nam-Trieu. The sea was calm, visibility good. After having assembled, the force proceeded to anchor and marry up its component parts, no mean feat considering that all this had to be done in the dark. *Béarn* off-loaded four LCAs, *Céphée* two, *Bételgeuse* two, using ships' own gear.

Force Z was then reformed into four task groups, each intended to be tailored to the tasks it was expected to face. An essentially cooperative landing was now possible, but precautions were taken. The leading groups were combat loaded, ammunition was carried:

- **First task group**: two minesweepers, six LCAs, and two sampans, with the mission of reconnoitering the Vu-Yen cut over to the Cua-Cam, occupying it, check sweeping it, and buoying it. According to terms of the Franco-Chinese accord, none of this work was to begin until daylight, although the task group could and did pull up to the cut while it was still dark.

- **Second task group**: six LCIs guided to the entrance by destroyer *Algérien*, to seize the airfield and port.

- **Third task group**: destroyer-leader *Triomphant* and two LSTs, to seize the naval station and yard. General Valluy—the troop commander—rode her; so did a civilian pilot (Pothin).

- **Fourth task group**: auxiliary cruiser/transport *Barfleur* and five merchant cargo ships, to unload administratively in the port.

There was in effect a fifth task group: the cruiser force and the fleet train. This was essentially a gunfire support and contingency group. Its *Emile-Bertin* flew the flags of both Leclerc and Auboyneau, too. It remained at the anchorage, ready to intervene as needed.

After the Vu-Yen cut was secure, the landing ships and craft of the second and third task groups were to pass through one after the other—in order—with those with the farthest to go passing first. The transports of the fourth group were to pass through only after an interval of one hour. Sweepers would precede all of the larger ships.

On arrival in the port, the larger ships were to tie up either at designated quays or to mooring buoys in the stream and to contact the Chinese authorities as to the unloading of their personnel and matériel. For those at buoys, landing craft would ferry their personnel ashore.[1]

REALITY STRIKES

That was the plan, already slightly modified in light of things that had happened or had not, in ways too byzantine to follow. But it is a military truism that no plan survives unchanged the first contact with the enemy. Neither did this one. We shall attempt to find our way through the major events, in any case, especially where they offer us something of use.

The major changes were made, of course, in light of several pieces of last-minute political and military news. The assumed regularization of relations with the Chinese led to an increased emphasis on giving Bentré more the appearance of a peaceful relief, effected not by troops on assault craft but rather on transports, coming ashore administratively at quays. Previous plans to occupy Haiphong's airfield were abandoned. So was the plan to seize Hongay. Bentré would appear at Haiphong in the form of LSTs, LCIs, larger warships, and transports only. Bir-Hacheim was scrubbed.

Participation by LCAs upriver was cancelled; they were to remain at the Vu-Yen cut, helping to secure it. Coming at the last minute as it did, this change raised hell with the reloading at Edouard.

Then the U.S. Navy made it known from Hong Kong that the

entrance to Haiphong could not be considered really clear. We had not fully swept those waters. The remaining mines were no doubt deep in the mud. *Triomphant* found a mine adrift on the 5th and sank it. So Auboyneau ordered a full-scale sweep—not just a light check sweep—of the channel before any ships displacing two thousand or more tons entered it. More time lost.

Then too, despite the Chunking accords, the French liaison group ashore began to have difficulties with Lu-Han and his staff. During the day of March 4, the Chinese at Hanoi seemed to want to contest one of the clauses of the accords. They indicated, however, that they would still issue instructions to Haiphong to permit the French to land on the 6th.

During the morning of the 5th, the Chinese at Haiphong appeared agreeable to the landing, but they had as yet received no orders on the subject from Hanoi. That evening they declared that, under these conditions, the landing would be opposed. They declined any responsibility for what happened before they received specific instructions from Hanoi.

Chinese staff work and communications were perhaps not all they could have been. Or perhaps for reasons best known to them, the Chinese needed more time before the French came in. Or there might just have been a last demonstration of who was really in charge, here. Or perhaps there was a combination of all of the above.

Leclerc decided not to put the operation on hold, in any case. Again orders were given not to respond to shore fire, no matter what, without direct approval from him. Ships and craft were to moor at their designated berths, but troops were not to debark until, again, the Chinese agreed.[2] The dice had been cast.

EXECUTION

During the early hours of March 6, then, the minesweepers and LCAs of the first task group landed a small commando detachment and sampans at the Vu-Yen cut, as planned. They soon cleared the cut up to the Cua-Cam. At daylight, everything was as ready for the next move as could be. Ashore, everything appeared quiet.

Out at Edouard, however, in the dark, there must have been feverish activity. Loading officers were making last-minute adjustments to loads, others were checking to see that whatever they had matched the latest modification to the plans. Troops prepared for a short run to shore.

The second wave, led to the cut by *Algérien*, now included two of the sweepers as well as the six LCIs. The minesweeping proved to be difficult and slow, holding up the third wave (*Triomphant* and the two LSTs)—all over two thousand tons—but the LCIs continued in.

At 0840 the LCIs began to receive fire from the shore—at first tentative, then heavy. *Triomphant* had by then passed the cut. Her captain (Jubelin) was the senior officer present afloat. She carried the troop commander aboard. Assuming the duties of OTC (officer in tactical command), she signaled the LCIs not to return the fire but to assemble on her. She herself began to receive fire.

By 0930 two of the LCIs had been put out of action. *Triomphant* moved up to the port entrance. Hit several times more, she fired two warning rounds from her main battery in the direction of a mortar. Shore fire let up.

Barfleur and the merchantmen of the fourth wave did not receive *Triomphant*'s order not to come through the cut. Passing through, they continued up the river. They made tempting targets. The Chinese (and the suspicion is, perhaps some of the onlooking local Viets) could not resist.

At 0948 fire from the shore reopened, strongly. Up to then, it had come mainly from machine guns and mortars. It was now clearly joined by that from artillery, light and heavy. Fire from the shore became intense. Casualties began to mount, damage to hurt.

One of Commentry's men, a former gunnery officer (Bernard Favin-Lévêque) was making the passage upriver on *Triomphant*, keeping out of the way. Gunnery control, above the bridge, took a hit. The ship's gunnery officer—a classmate—was killed at his post. At a glance from the captain, Favin-Lévêque removed the gun boss's body and took his place. Without a pause, he announced, "This is Lieutenant Favin-Lévêque, assuming the functions of director of fire." Circuits were checked and readiness reported. Fire from the shore continued heavy.

General Valluy on board *Triomphant* authorized return of this new fire, and Admiral Auboyneau on *Emile-Bertin* confirmed the order. French twenty-millimeter and forty-millimeter automatic guns opened up first, soon joined by 138s. They immediately cleared the river banks. Firing let up.

Nonetheless the French were in an untenable position. Two out of the six LCIs had been shot up and were dead in the Cam's muddy water. They were no longer prepared for an assault landing. The next move was up to the brass. Meanwhile, they closed up.

Triomphant was designed for gun and torpedo warfare on the high seas. She carried no armor but made a relatively large target on the constricted Cua-Cam. It was her guns that covered the force. Unable to maneuver, she herself took many hits.

On hearing the sounds of firing upriver, the LCAs left at the cut on their own initiative came up to see what they could do. There was not much—they carried only light weapons—but the LCAs fell to with combat evacuation of the wounded. They saved the lives of many of the wounded, this way.

Emile-Bertin at Edouard had also been receiving fire, theirs coming from the coastal battery active at Appowan. It finally forced the flagship to shift her anchorage. She then returned the fire, silencing it. Nothing more was heard from those guns. But *Emile-Bertin* was busy monitoring the activity ashore.

Meanwhile, *Triomphant* ordered a general reversal of course, back down the river. For the smaller landing craft this was no problem, but for the big, fat underpowered merchantmen it was. Two ran aground and had to be pulled off. *Triomphant* successfully shepherded them all down to a temporary anchorage just above the cut. There they paused to see what came next.[3]

CEASE-FIRE AND TERMS

Ashore, the two designated French liaison officers finally succeeded in locating the Chinese staff. Reaching their quay, a rapid conference was held. Between them, it was agreed to send a Franco-Chinese team of negotiators out to *Triomphant* to work out the terms of a cease-fire. There, after more discussion and reference to their respective commanders, a general cease-fire was issued, effective on both sides. This one stuck.

At 1200, *Triomphant* and the transports were anchored in the Cua-Cam. *Gazelle*, with Leclerc and Auboyneau aboard, joined them there at 1240. *Savorgnan-de-Brazza* meanwhile took aboard the dead and wounded from the LCIs. The toll had been heavy—twenty-six dead, including twelve seamen (seven from the LCIs and five from *Triomphant*).

The negotiators returned ashore. Only at 2200, however, was final agreement reached. The general cease-fire was confirmed. But in the midst of a culture that placed great importance on "face," the terms accepted by the French were hard ones. Even so, Haiphong's quays were alit all night with burning Chinese munitions.

Under the agreed terms, the French were again given permission to land, but to save Chinese face only after a preliminary evacuation of the river by the French to below the cut. Even then, only on the 7th—the next day—and only on the island of Haly, just upstream from the city, called the island of the dead.

With *Triomphant* organizing the movements, on the 7th *Barfleur*, three merchantmen (two of which had to be pulled off the mud), the amphibious ships, and *Triomphant* returned through the cut. By 1135 they were all anchored again in the river.

Actual debarking at Haiphong began on the morning of the 8th. At 1000, *Barfleur* entered Haiphong port, followed by the LSTs and cargo ships. There *Triomphant* turned her responsibilities as officer in tactical command over to *Fantasque* and *Savorgnan-de-Brazza*.[4]

Triomphant headed for an anchorage in Along Bay. She counted some 439 holes in her superstructure, all made by hostile machine guns, mortars, and artillery. She had earned a breather, for sure.

Overall French losses during the engagement were twenty-six dead and perhaps one hundred wounded. Two LCIs were put out of action.

With everything now returned to normalcy, on March 10, *Béarn* headed for Saigon to hospitalize the wounded. The other ships joined *Triomphant* in Along Bay. There with full honors, the dead were interred on one of the small islands found everywhere in the bay. *Mort pour la France.*

OUTCOME

Not until March 16, however, did Lu-Han allow the first of Leclerc's troops to enter Hanoi, the main body not entering until the 18th. From then on, the relief went more smoothly. The Viet-Minh in the accords of the 6th had assented to this; if nothing else, it assured the departure of the Chinese. So there was no difficulty with them. Commentry, once again back in the citadel, took over the functions of COMAR Tonkin as before.

On March 24 in Along Bay *Emile-Bertin* was passed in review before the entire Bentré fleet. On board the cruiser taking the salute were Admiral d'Argenlieu, President Ho (he had been received with full honors), and General Leclerc.

On March 26 General Lu-Han was received by d'Argenlieu aboard the flagship in his turn and given lunch. This proved to be the old *Marine*'s last manifestation of splendor, its "last hurrah."

After this, Force Z was dissolved. Auboyneau's big ships returned one by one to Saigon. By May, only the cruiser *Emile-Bertin* and the destroyer-leader *Fantasque* were left up north. One of their assignments was to pick up the remaining French stranded in Shanghai and Petchili and bring them down south. The other big ships gradually returned to Toulon—to be laid up, then broken up.[5]

Bentré represented the end of an era, in many ways. In June 1946 Commentry was brought home to PREMAR Trois at Toulon. Promoted rear admiral in July 1946, he was retired in October of that year. Gone was "le Vieux Charles," or even "Blanche-

Neige." He too. *Kontum* took a mine at Cape Saint-Jacques that same year and sank.

WHAT NOW?

Indochina, from a purely parochial naval point of view, served one good, at least. It quickly wore off most of the schism within the now reintegrated regular Navy. The undermanned and shorthanded French needed each other too much for there to be room for that sort of thing. The "Grand Corps' " professionalism pulled it through.

But there was another good: the development of what became the *dinassauts*. Admittedly, they did not spring fully completed—finished in all respects—from a single moment of history, but rather they represented history and technology combining to meet a current need. Most progress does. The Americans were to pick up on the idea twenty years later.

Lu-Han's army group was officially redeployed from Haiphong to Manchuria at the end of April by a force of twenty-seven U.S. Navy LSTs. Even then, a few small Chinese units remained in Indochina, and there were continual reports of scattered armed clashes between them and Leclerc's men. It was actually the end of August before the last of Lu-Han's men were gone.

D'Argenlieu now had only to turn the Saigon-Hanoi accord of March 6 into reality. But that is postexpeditionary, another story. It is epilogue.

NOTES

1. Jacques Michel, ed., *La Marine Française en Indochine de 1939 à 1955* (Vincennes: Service Historique de la Marine, 1973), II (Août 1945–Decembre 1946), pp. 165–66; Bernard Favin-Lévêque, *Souvenirs de Mer et d'Ailleurs* (Versailles: Editions des 7 Vents, 1990), pp. 133–34.

2. Lévêque, pp. 136–37; Jean Gabrié, *Les Marines de la Guerre 1935–1945* (Vincennes: Service Historique de la Marine, 1994), pp. 113–14.
3. Michel, pp. 174–79; Lévêque, pp. 138–42; Gabrié, pp. 114–15.
4. Michel, pp. 194–95; Gabrié, p. 116.
5. Michel, pp. 195; Gabrié, p. 118.

9

EPILOGUE

OPPORTUNITY

Modern military power—in the form of CEEO—had by April 1946 created for France in Indochina a real window of political opportunity. It was not even then certain that meaningful relations with Ho Chi Minh were possible, but to the clearheaded the alternative—a "people's war" and military pacification for years to come—was unthinkable. Absolutely. Exhausted itself from war, occupation, and liberation, France needed peace at least as much as its colony.

Ho had, after all, already agreed in principle to a Republic of Vietnam within an Indo-Chinese federation, a member of the new French Union. Or so he said. But what did that—and Ho—really mean? The Saigon-Hanoi accord was a very general one.

D'Argenlieu himself met Ho for the first time on March 24, off Haiphong on board *Emile-Bertin*. There they opened preliminary discussions on the actual meaning of the March 6 accord, trying to spell out the details. Negotiations continued for the next six months, at Dalat, Camranh, and Fontainebleau (Paris). The French defended their ultimate sovereignty and public order. Ho made propaganda, especially in Paris.

Ho understood the idea of "making peace to go forward." It was at best only a tactical move, in which to gain a better position for whatever came next. In Indochina he continued his armed propaganda, exterminating his opposition. When d'Argenlieu took the police measures necessary to protect the people from Ho, Ho charged that d'Argenlieu was "taking prisoners" and "undermining democratic liberties." Large sections of the French public swallowed this whole.

BMEO

There is a kind of postscript to all this. The role of the major fleet units in the recovery of Indochina was indeed by and large done, well done. The old, graceful Navy "in white" was being sent home and paid off. But the new, ugly small craft (the Navy "in khaki") still had work to do. Lots of it.

Having been established in Haiphong, then in Hanoi, it quickly became apparent that in the absence of further amphibious operations, the *Marine*'s essential role had become waterways security. This was true in all of Tonkin, but particularly on the Lach-Tray—Canal of Bamboos—Red River route between Haiphong and Hanoi. BMEO was given the task.

The first convoys up here were organized early in April 1946. By early July they ran two or three per week, some of LCTs, others of towed barges, even of junks poling or under sail, all of French interest. BMEO provided either escort LCAs or armed guards, or sometimes both, with reinforcements on call.

By August, BMEO had organized and escorted eighteen convoys carrying some five thousand tons of cargo. Lost in this time was only a single junk, by accident, part of whose cargo was saved. Not one vessel was lost to rebel action. This task was to last for nine years, way past the dissolution of BMEO.

EPILOGUE

REALITY

As the negotiations between Ho and the French progressed, two major points of difference began to emerge. One of these concerned the future status of Cochin-China. The Chinese (and Japanese) either going or gone, Ho stiffened his negotiating position. All three Kys were to be unified under Hanoi. The south was now to have no choice in this. The French on the other hand could not abandon their colony.

There was also the question of the status of the future Vietnamese Army. Ho apparently saw a military coexistence, side by side, until after the five-year drawdown set out in the accord. Then except for a few permanent sea and air bases the French were in effect to be gone. No longer dominated by the Gaullists, Paris remained willing to see what amounted to a Vietnamese constabulary, but all national defense and foreign affairs had to remain under French control. Paris would not draw down its forces. It told d'Argenlieu to get tough.

The two parties talked all through the spring and summer, getting nowhere. The determined and western had met the determined and byzantine. It was Ho who wanted to transfer the talks to Paris. When negotiations there stalled, too, in September, Ho tried to appeal over the government's head to the communists, who formed one-third of the French electorate, and to the liberal press. In October Ho finally returned to Hanoi, angry, hands empty.[1]

POLITICS VIET STYLE

Meanwhile, there was no peace in Indochina. Ho kept the pressure on. The Viet-Minh used this time to eliminate the considerable armed forces of the noncommunist nationalist party known as the Dai-Viet. Agitprop—propaganda designed to stir people up—continued unceasingly, night and day. As early as April, Ho's men had ambushed a road convoy bringing the crew of a French naval patrol plane into Haiphong from Cat-Bi airfield. The following months witnessed the first attacks against river convoys running between Haiphong and Hanoi.

On May 30 d'Argenlieu recognized a Republic of Cochin-China based on the colonial structure as a provisionally sovereign state. D'Argenlieu's recognition here was contingent upon a referendum in the south, on the holding of which both sides had already agreed. All this did was to further anger Ho. His writ did not always run in the south. Yet.

Meanwhile, the *Marine* and Army were reestablishing French authority in population centers like Hongay and Campha, along the northeastern coast of Tonkin.

Within Haiphong and Hanoi, Giap began to erect blockhouses, barricades, and other works in key locations, a step that Leclerc periodically resisted. Early in August, Giap's troops ambushed a supply convoy near Hanoi, inflicting fifty-two casualties.

In Cochin-China, a new wave of political assasssination, ambushes, and river mining was reported, even there.[2]

French General Valluy understood that existing strength in the north (drawn down to thirteen thousand troops, now) required that he work to keep the troubles localized, that with his forces he could not hope to handle a generalized conflict. Working against time and with limited resources, Giap now counted some thirty thousand regulars in the north alone, supported by ten thousand Tu-Ve (militia). In his attempt Valluy failed, for reasons well beyond his control.

HAIPHONG

With Ho—who had tried negotiation—back, the whole nonwar was obviously reaching a crisis. To get what he wanted now clearly required war. But it had to be a war in which the Viets had to be seen as the injured, innocent party, and the French as murderers of the people. A ready-made issue was at hand.

Control of customs was the issue. In developing countries, customs is a symbol of independence as well as—the income tax being unheard of—a major source of revenue. To dry up this source of

EPILOGUE

Viet funds—and incidentally to cut off the smuggling in of arms—in October the French at Haiphong seized control of customs. FNEO at the same time established patrols to cut off Viet supplies coming in clandestinely by water.

On November 20 a small French patrol LCA seized a Chinese sampan carrying contraband cargo. The rebels reacted by firing on the customs launch as it was bringing in its prize and by setting up roadblocks in the city. Leclerc bulldozed the roadblocks down. Heavy fighting ensued, dying out only the next day. The trap was set.

Colonel Debès, commander of French troops in Haiphong, was now authorized to use all means at his disposal to make himself complete master of the city. He issued an ultimatum demanding that Giap evacuate specific sections of the city. It was ignored, of course. The Viets wanted him to attack them.

On November 23, therefore, on orders, *Savorgnan-de-Brazza* opened fire on specific rebel positions, as did *Chevreuil* and later *Dumont-d'Urville*. By the 27th, French ground and naval forces had ejected the enemy from the city, and serious fighting ceased. For this, Debès paid with twenty dead and thirty wounded. Viet propaganda claimed that many thousands of innocent lives had been taken, and made the most of the opportunity this offered.

According to this propaganda, the French had indiscriminately shelled native quarters of the city, even using a cruiser. In the course of the fighting, perhaps several hundred Annamese could have been killed; Viet propaganda claimed as many as six thousand. The trap had been sprung.[3]

HANOI

On December 19, better prepared, Giap unleashed a general attack on the garrisons of Tonkin—except Hongay—and Cochin-China. All positions were held, not without losses. All roads and waterways, however, were cut, and all lines of communication—especially in the north—had to be reopened. Apparently, Giap was ready to test conclusions with the French, either running them back to the coast and keeping them there or continuing the fight from the brush.

In Hanoi, the Viets attempted a lightning *coup de force*. At 2000, bands of rebels cut off electricity and water and attacked both French military personnel and civilians. With the civilians, the Viets resorted to the now-familiar tactic of riot, pillage, torture, and rape. Nevertheless, due in part to a last-minute warning from intelligence sources, Leclerc after several days of heavy fighting reestablished order. The city was under martial law. Troops patrolled the streets.

Unlike the Haiphong affair of the previous month, which remained an essentially isolated incident, the Viet's attempted coup this time was accompanied by similar outbreaks elsewhere in Tonkin as well as in Cochin-China. Smaller battles took place in a dozen towns north of Hanoi (to run the French out) and on the coast at places like Hué and Tourane (to pin down potential reserves). They all failed. A war that was to last eight years was now under way, with no turning back on either side.

None of France's military skill, none of the brave deeds, none of the blood was going to change a thing. Ultimately, France was to lose that war.

Leclerc now came north in full force. There would be no peace. Leclerc's troops ran Ho's forces off into the brush, again. Ho went into the Viet-Bac hills on the Chinese border. These he made his primary politico-military base for the rest of what had now become truly a "people's war."[4]

CEEO DISSOLVED

December 1946 also saw the organizational acknowledgment that the expeditionary phase of the recovery of Indochina was over. Foreseen now were no more major campaigns. These were being replaced by pacification, backed by minor skirmishes between small units. Paris looked to paying more attention to the wider Far East now. Reorganization reflected this.

Auboyneau remained Commander Naval Forces Far East in overall command. While still building on history, Far East Naval Forces (FNEO) was, however, more clearly split in two. There was now a Commander Naval Division Far East who "owned" the main fleet units in the area down to but not including 288-foot LSTs.

Commander Naval Forces Indochina (*Marine Indochine*) remained. He it was who "owned" the khaki navy. This totaled now approximately one hundred craft ranging in size from 120-foot LCTs to 41-foot LCAs as well as patrol boats, minesweepers, and myriad small native sampans and junks.

BMEO was abolished as such. In the beginning, its *Fusiliers* freed towns and cleared whole provinces. They now were reduced to being cops, not as they saw it, fighters, called on for backup in a high risk arrest or the ratissage (security sweep) of a suspect village. Otherwise they worked as routine patrols. Their mere presence was often enough to prevent trouble of any kind. The *Fusiliers* were therefore integrated in a newly organized Amphibious Force, part of Naval Forces Indochina.

Amphibious Force was broken into two amphibious groups, one in Tonkin and one in Cochin-China. These amphibious groups each included an amphibious flotilla, coastal posts, river posts, and a base. Each formed an administrative unit. Posts monitored maritime traffic. They defended themselves. They reinforced boat crews. The old river flotillas meantime metamorphosed, splitting now into (officially) *dinassauts*, integral units of landing craft and crews married permanently with commandos. There were five of these *dinassauts* assigned in the north, to unruly Tonkin, and two to more pacified Cochin-China.

This reorganization better reflected the naval assets available to Commander FNEO, Indo-Chinese geography, and politico-military reality. The navy in white was still there, but the navy in khaki had carved for itself a more comfortable place in the organizational charts. When CEEO first arrived, these assets were not even a part of it.[5]

NOISES OFFSTAGE

Back in 1940, when the undeclared war between French Indochina and Thailand (then still known as Siam) had broken out, Thailand—Japan's puppet, also eager to capitalize on France's defeat in Europe—laid claim to large areas of Cambodia and Laos along the right bank of the Mekong. Bangkok's fleet was soundly defeated in the subsequent (January 1941) naval battle of Koh-Chang, but Tokyo backed its ally, to the point of demonstrating navally off the region to make its point. Hanoi was forced to give in, surrendering the contested areas.

At the beginning of 1946, having reasserted its place in Indochina, France demanded that Siam return the territories it had seized in 1941. Washington and London both offered Paris their support in this. Siam did all it could to draw out the question. It organized intensive propaganda in support of a plebiscite. It even provoked incidents. An accord between Paris and Bangkok was finally concluded at Washington in November. In it the lost areas were all given back. *Status quo ante bellum.*

NAM-DINH

When Giap attempted his Hanoi *coup de force* in December, Nam-Dinh—with a population of perhaps 70,000—was the third largest city in the north. It was located in the delta southeast of Hanoi, just off the Red River. Nam-Dinh was garrisoned by some five hundred troops. There was a French civilian population of around 250. Evacuation of these civilians and reinforcement of the isolated garrison became urgent.

A naval relief flotilla consisting of two LCTs, one LCI, and four LCMs entered the Red River at its mouth, expecting to arrive in the city via the narrow Nam-Dinh canal at dawn on January 6. Some four hundred airborne troops were scheduled to drop some hours earlier, to set up beachheads on the city side of the canal, ready for the flotilla's use.

As the flotilla approached Nam-Dinh, it met with heavy enemy fire, losing one LCM and its commanding officer. The cooperating airborne force ran into heavy AA fire, became widely scattered, and was unable to secure the intended beachhead areas.

The flotilla therefore landed on the far side of the canal, supported by gunfire from the landing craft. From there, they silenced the opposite bank and crossed over. By 1630, Nam-Dinh cleared.

EPILOGUE   113

The flotilla headed back, taking a number of French civilians with it.

Thereafter, there were regular convoys to Nam-Dinh, but these recurring convoys tied up *Fusiliers* and craft that could have been better used offensively elsewhere in the north. For the *Marine*, this was the shape of things to come.

RESIGNATION

As High Commissioner, Thierry d'Argenlieu was the one key to a realistic, enlightened, negotiated future for Indochina. Aristocratic, difficult, he was undoubtedly also a gallant sailor, a leading figure of the Church, and one of the passionate Frenchmen. An authentic Gaullist, de Gaulle trusted him. He knew de Gaulle's mind. Saigon is a long way from Paris. Communications were not the best. D'Argenlieu had been forced by circumstances to make on his own authority a number of hard political choices, only notifying Paris after the fact. He had literally at the last minute hammered out the March 6 Saigon-Hanoi accord under which Ho had accepted the French back into the north. Politics is, after all, the art of the possible—and compromise.

But de Gaulle had resigned in January 1946. He was followed by a whole parade of new leaders, none of whom had de Gaulle's vision of the future. There was no longer the same rapport between the *métropole* and Saigon. The gap between them widened, particularly over interpretations of the March 6 accord.

The events of December 1946 finished d'Argenlieu. After the situation fell apart, Paris abandoned him, left him "swinging in the breeze." In March 1947 d'Argenlieu, too, offered his resignation and quietly returned to his religious order. Indochina's last hope for an enlightened peace was gone. Ho and Giap had turned the expedition's military success into political defeat—thirty years and more later, that much is clear.

NOTES

1. Georges Thierry d'Argenlieu, *Chronique d'Indochine 1945–1947* (Paris: Editions Albin Michel, 1985), pp. 217–361.

2. Ibid., p. 333, table of incidents.
3. Jacques Michel, ed., *La Marine Française en Indochine de 1939 à 1955* (Vincennes: Service Historique de la Marine, 1973), II (Août 1945–Decembre 1946), pp. 28, 255–61; D'Argenlieu, pp. 349–61.
4. Michel, pp. 29, 271–73; D'Argenlieu, pp. 363–92.
5. Michel, pp. 240–44, 295–97; Robert Kilian, *History and Memories: The Naval Infantrymen in Indochina* (Paris: Editions Berger-Levrault, 1948), passim.

CONCLUSION

THE JAPANESE LEGACY

In Indochina, the defeated Japanese in 1945 left the French a Viet-Minh-led skeleton rebel government already in place, gathering to itself the reins of power. This government had to be either ousted or dealt with, accommodating to the people's nationalist aspirations, at least. The Gaullists sent out Thierry d'Argenlieu, who tried dealing with it and ended up fighting it.

At this point, except when it occasionally tested its strength against the French, the Viet-Minh spent their time building up their politico-military infrastructure. Leclerc fought the rebels, his victories marked by Viet dead. The Viets brought the people under their control, their victories marked by the heads of village notables on sticks in the square.

Even the early riots were part of a cool, premeditated revolutionary pattern. These riots were not just to terrorize the French and their allies. That they did, but there was more.

The Viets always had a reason for things like this within their revolutionary theory. There was no allowable waste.

It was and is relatively simple—using what the communists call "agitprop" (a careful combination of agitation and propaganda)—to get a mob stirred up and howling, and then to loot and rape. After this has happened, those involved tend to feel somehow guilty and a part of the revolution, no matter what—if any—their original political convictions might have been. Not so simple is the groundwork required to set all this up. This takes time.

The first Gaullist political emissary to arrive in the south—Cedile—tried for a month to make meaningful political contact with the Nam-Bo in Saigon. Finally admitting defeat, he announced that the Viet-Minh were incapable even of keeping order, and he therefore appealed to Gracey to step in. The basic assumption was almost certainly not true. The Viets could have kept order. It was just as certain that they did not want to. They were using those riots as a political tool. When d'Argenlieu arrived, he took over from there. It was not yet necessarily too late, but the clock was running, both in Saigon and in Paris.

NAVAL FORCES

If we are talking about overseas expeditionary forces—and most go overseas—navies are involved. To all that followed, the *Marine* contributed transport; big ship, big-gun fire support; *dinassauts* for riverine and estuarine warfare; continued supply. It contributed its sloops and its landing parties. It threw in an embryo naval air arm for good measure. It would have been sorely missed.

FNEO was not technically a part of CEEO. Rather, it was under d'Argenlieu's operational control for the recovery of Indochina, cooperating with Leclerc. Surprisingly no one stood on his dignity at any point, as far as we know. Commentry's name was well received in both camps.

Throughout the entire expedition, Paris by definition represented a Western maritime state, Hanoi an Oriental land one. Paris constructed CEEO as a European army corps—three divisions, one of them armored—to be transported to the scene of battle by sea, supported by the fleet during a landing, then turned loose. That is not the way things worked out at all.

CONCLUSION

The battlefield was two large river deltas and a mountain chain, none of them suited to the large-scale use of either infantry or armor. In the deltas, as a rule, small bodies of troops were moved on landing craft along waterways, executing a series of miniature amphibious assaults as they went. There was no other way they could go.

The mountainous areas were no better for armor. The burden of pacification fell again on the rifleman, on foot, here. The Navy could give little support, so things progressed only slowly.

Against this, Hanoi had little more than large amounts of manpower. It laid crude but effective mines in the waterways, built barricades, and set up ambushes. Every so often it massed some of this overwhelming manpower against a small French outpost, overran it, then disappeared again.

Though smaller forces can operate for a time from offshore ships, except for those countries with effectively unlimited maritime resources, most cannot. Expeditions of any size require a nearby overseas base. These can be seized in a preliminary move. They can be provided from one's own resources. Or they can be seized by an ally. Such was the case, in effect, with Saigon. Saigon was seized by the British, and only turned over to the French after a sufficient buildup of French forces. The French then used the south as a base from which to seize Hanoi.

None of this could have happened without what we call today sea control and force projection, across the seas, along the coasts, and up rivers. The *Marine* would have been sorely missed here. No expedition would have been possible without it, even though the recovery of Indochina was primarily an Army matter.

THE SEA VERSUS THE LAND

It should be remembered that we are talking here to a significant army-corps-sized expedition. Most will be an infantry division or more in size. Ninety-five percent of what they use will have to come by sea. Back in 1945 and 1946, France had to move almost one hundred percent by sea. With no significant disposable merchantmen under its own control, Paris had to use *la Royale* for this, too.

The *Marine* came to Indochina essentially with the remnants of its pre–World War II blue-water fleet. It was prepared for the wrong war. The one it actually fought involved sloops, landing ships, and craft, not battleships and cruisers. It used *Fusiliers Marins* and landing parties, not fifteen-inch guns, on rivers and canals, not blue water. But being a navy, it took to amphibious warfare with ease—enough of them did, at any rate. They improvised. They found the landing ships and craft locally—in Singapore, in Manila.

The Chinese with their overwhelming numbers of ground troops and artillery were able to dominate limited areas of the sea off Haiphong, as well as the rivers, as long as they were in the north. The French were able to dominate the land from the sea at all other times, as far as their guns and *dinassauts* could reach. Without aircraft carriers, however, they were limited beyond that. "From the Sea . . . ," please note.

The expedition's ground operations won their greatest successes when they remained within range of their seaborne support. The distances inland involved have lengthened since 1945–1946, but naval gunfire support and the mobility their ships and craft provided were absolutely necessary, even sometimes just to survive.

Weather, hydrography, tides, and currents did on the other hand impose continual restrictions on French strategy and tactics. The Army-dominated staff did not, it is reported, always submit gracefully to this. But submit they did. In combined operations in country like this, acceptable alternatives did not exist. This the *Marine* had to prove, however, and did, early.

THE DECISIVE FAILURE

France's return to Indochina, even in battalion strength, was delayed from August 1945 to October 1945. Even then, it came only with British help. Paris's time in the Annamite Kys ran out somewhere in this time. Even then, the French did not unseat Ho until

CONCLUSION

six months later. Ho remained in Hanoi long enough to establish a government coherent even when forced back under ground.

Ho had seized the nationalist mantle. He was unscrupulous enough to hide behind it while he used the tools of his communist ideology to destroy his nationalist allies. He used his time to organize his Viet-Minh, propagandize, and destroy Paris's image. It had all gone too far by the time Leclerc arrived in force, even in Saigon.

On announcement of the Japanese capitulation, the average *nhaqué* expected to see a French squadron tie up at once at the Quai d'Argonne, but none came. France was beaten, the Viet-Minh whispered. France had no more ships. France will not come back. As the story goes, one of the French wives who came to the Quai d'Argonne to greet *Triomphant* showed her off to an Annamese servant, "Look, there are still French ships." The servant replied, "That is not a French ship, she is American!" To which the wife replied, "Look at the flag." The answer came, "The flag is French, the ship is not; the Americans just loaned her to you for a week." This went on and on.

In the 1880s, Jules Ferry (*le Tonkinois*) had dreamed of a French Pacific empire, with Indochina being the centerpiece. This was the end of that dream. It took ten more years to work that out, however. Whisper by whisper.

Everything considered, it seems that if in 1945 Decoux had been allowed to continue the only practicable policy—neutrality—open to a helpless, isolated Indochina, the French could probably have avoided the Japanese *coup de force* of March. With peace, if France had insisted that Decoux be immediately released and restored as Governor General; if *les anciens* had been released from internment and prison and rearmed, to back him up; and if the French had spoken with one voice right at the beginning, there would have been no hiatus of French authority for as long as there was. This was probably the crucial gap.

In this, the British had been helpful allies. But having to come back to Indochina behind the British did not help the French image, either. The French were inevitably made to look weak, incapable of ruling by themselves any longer. The continual turmoil in Saigon did nothing to change that. Hanoi came too late.

LESSONS FROM INDOCHINA

The "lessons" from Indochina are that under conditions such as were faced in 1945 and 1946, a modern military expedition will almost certainly be able to land and carry out its military tasks, its immediate ones. But even in the midst of its tactical "wins," the local opposition will begin to undermine the force's role. Everything the troops do will be turned against them. Underground propaganda will lead to sabotage and terror. If the expedition remains long enough, organized, armed guerrillas will appear. At home, congressional and public support will be undermined in every way.

Every expedition has its allocated political time. Whatever it achieves has to be accomplished before that time runs out. Run out time will. This makes the politico-military interface at the field level of overriding importance. This interface reaches down farther than it used to, too. That you may not have heard, yet.

This political time can be extended by placing the expedition within political cover at all levels—international, national, and local. CEEO's effort has strong international aspects involving Britain, the United States, China, the Netherlands, even Japan right from the start. Allied support was essential, even if sometimes a restraint. Such support must be lined up beforehand, even at considerable cost in precious time and effort. The press is always a two-edged tool, but if it is not kept informed, it will invent its own story. At the local—force—level much can be done here.

This situation is aggravated if one heads an international effort. Thankfully, such was not the case with CEEO. Leclerc commanded only French forces. Mountbatten and Gracey got out as soon as they decently could.

Hurry. Hurry. Show maximum force that evening and open the market in the morning. French Marshal Lyautey—who kept order in barely pacified Morocco during World War I with five battalions—was right.

CONCLUSION

Senior leadership must be on the ground early. D'Argenlieu took too long to take over in Saigon. Leclerc was there earlier but not soon enough. He was in any case Genesuper, not directly responsible for political affairs.

INTELLIGENCE

If you are overwhelmingly the stronger, you can ignore your enemy, going wherever and doing whatever you want. That can be expensive, but it is possible. In situations like Indochina, that is not likely to be the case. The opposition will have overwhelming manpower and knowledge of the ground. The expedition will always be the fewer, with only some technological advantage. In a sense, expeditionary warfare is first of all a battle of intelligence services.

Any one strong nonrational affirmation—communism, yes, but also nationalism and religion, even tribalism—is sufficient to justify the organization and discipline required by such a resistance. Most often, nationalism combines with one of the other first two. Indochina demonstrates that any expedition must be politically deft, ready to counter this. The object of the campaign is not just to collect a number of tactical wins, but also to end up where and how you want to be.

Good intelligence is a must—not only military but also political. It is not possible to guard against everything all the time. Intelligence tells you what you must do. Leclerc was well served by his intelligence in the north, in Hanoi, in December 1946. It was partly this that enabled him to hang on there then.

Good intelligence is a necessary ingredient of deft, effective psychological warfare ("psywar"), too. Psywar will be waged on both sides, and in this the enemy is apt to be very good. Lacking any technological advantage, they will exploit what they have. Every mistake we make, every defeat will be magnified; every good deed, every victory explained away.

It might be useful in this regard to remember that even though we are not colonialists, we are usually painted by our enemies as being neocolonialists, whatever they are. If at all possible, we will be made to look just like the French, every time. Mere good intentions alone are no defense, at any time.

FAILURE IS AN ORPHAN

The French in the end were trapped by their own success. They could not negotiate from weakness. They, on the other hand, could not bring themselves to make the necessary concessions once they were strong. They had to believe that political power grew out of the barrel of a gun. Their own recent history should have shown them the limits of such an idea.

France's failure in Indochina was primarily a political one. By the end of 1946, its expedition to recover Indochina had done its job, with élan and sometimes incredible bravery. The tricolor once again flew all over. Except as limited by the Viet-Minh, Paris's writ again ran from Cape Camau to Moncay.

But Ho had not been either captured or killed. The Viet-Minh were not stamped out.

Overall accommodation to postwar internal political reality—as laid out at Brazzaville—could not be had. D'Argenlieu (and Paris) never worked that one out.

Military victory buys time. It can under certain circumstances even modify terms. That is all. In the time thus gained, short of annihilation, it is a political (compromise) solution that must be found. When Ho Chi Minh returned from Paris in October 1946 as he did—angry, insulted—the war die was cast.

"LESSONS" FROM THE VAULT

This history is now ended. To write history simply to record events is a sterile business. History needs to be used—for what it shows us others have tried, how they did it, and the results. France's 1945–1946 expedition to Indochina is loaded with such data. Read it, please. We are going to need it.

One can always be more objective about things that happened

CONCLUSION

some time in the past, to others and in far-off places. The period covered here is now a while ago, in case you have not noticed. Official histories dealing with this expedition began appearing in the 1970s, and personal memoirs in the 1980s. We can by this time put together a pretty good mosaic not only of what happened but also of how and why.

One hears that the JCS has assumed the position today (1996) that it would not support any intervention anywhere unless the United States could bring overwhelming strength to bear. That would be nice. Lots of luck! But . . .

For the United States, forward presence, readiness, pre-positioned equipment, and supplies are going to be critical. There will not be time to finish training half-ready reserves, to design and build inshore and river minesweepers and patrol boats, or anything else. To be unready is to guarantee that any crisis will get out of hand, as in Indochina.

That story is here set out, for us all, as best I can. Read it, weep, and be not surprised when it all comes around again, for us this time, east of Suez. Our experiences in the Persian Gulf during the late 1980s and early 1990s have got to be the exception, not the rule.

APPENDIXES

Appendix A

SUMMARY OF THE PROVISIONS OF THE DECLARATION OF THE FRENCH PROVISIONAL GOVERNMENT DATED MARCH 24, 1945, CONCERNING INDOCHINA

After the war, the French community will form a French Union, to include France, an Indo-Chinese Federation, and others, whose external relations will be represented by France. Within that union, Indochina will be free. Within that union, without discrimination as to race, religion, or origin, and according to merit, the Indo-Chinese will have access to every post.

The five-state Indo-Chinese Federation will have its own federal government presided over by a governor general and ministers responsible to him. These will be chosen from among the Indo-Chinese and resident French. Under him, will be an appointed council of state, charged with preparing the laws. An elected assembly will vote the taxes, approve the laws, and advise on commercial treaties.

Freedom of the press, association, assembly, thought, and belief will form the basis of Indo-Chinese law.

With the help of the *métropole* and within a general system of defense for the union, the Indo-Chinese Federation will organize, train, and equip ground, naval, and air forces, within which the Indo-Chinese will have equal access to all ranks, on the basis of merit.

Political, economic, and social progress will be encouraged at every level. The federation will enjoy an economic autonomy permitting it to attain its full potential in agriculture, industry, and commerce.

With peace, Indochina will be free to develop its own commercial relations with all other countries, particularly China.

Indochina's fundamental statute will be finalized after consultations with qualified bodies of a liberated Indochina.

Paris, March 24, 1945

Appendix B

SUMMARY OF KEY PROVISIONS OF FRANCO-VIETNAMESE COMPLEMENTARY MILITARY ACCORD OF APRIL 3, 1946

1. Franco-Vietnamese forces relieving the Chinese will consist of ten thousand Vietnamese troops and fifteen thousand French.
2. The ten thousand Vietnamese—five thousand of them armed—will be at the disposition of the French commanding general for the purposes of the relief, assisted by a Vietnamese liaison unit.
3. The French will not exceed fifteen thousand in number and will, except for five hundred colonials who may be used to guard Japanese POWs, be metropolitan French.
4. Carriage of arms when not on duty is in principle forbidden.
5. Roads and waterways are open to military traffic. Movements will not, however, be made without prior coordination with the Vietnamese government.
6. A central mixed liaison and control commission is created, seated at Hanoi.

7. Local mixed commissions will be set up, as needed, subordinate to the central one.
8. French troops are provisionally to be located as follows:

Location	Number
Hanoi	5,000 including 1,000 at the air base
Haiphong	1,750
Hongay	1,025
Nam-Dinh, Hue, Tourane	825 each
frontier region—Moncay, Langson, Caobang, Laokay, Laichau, Hagiang	2,775
other	1,475

General Salan   *Vo-Nguyen-Giap*   *Vu-Hong-Kanh*

Done at Hanoi

Appendix C

INDOCHINA 1945–1946 ERA LANDING CRAFT IN SERVICE

1. **Landing Craft, Assault (LCA)**
   dimensions/displacement: 12.5 meters × 3.5 meters/13 tons
   draft: 0.7 meters (laden)
   speed: 7 knots (2 gasoline engines)
   Small British-designed craft capable of carrying a squad of men under arms for short distances. No vehicles. Two machine guns. Some side armor. Used for commando assaults and as escorts/scouts for larger craft.
2. **Landing Craft, Vehicle and Personnel (LCVP)**
   dimensions/displacement: 12.5 meters × 3.5 meters/13 tons
   draft: 1.2 meters (laden)
   speed: 7.5 knots (2 diesels)
   Small U.S.-designed craft capable of carrying one Jeep or as many as twenty men. Noisy. No armament, no armor. Used for support tasks.
3. **Landing Craft, Mechanized (LCM)**
   dimensions/displacement: 50 feet × 14 feet/36 tons

draft: 1.3 meters (laden)
speed: 8 knots

Capable of carrying a maximum of 120 men or equivalent cargo (one GMC 2½-ton truck). Two machine guns.

4. **Gressier Barge ("cuirassé de rivière")**
dimensions/displacement: 31.0 meters × 6.5 meters/220 tons
draft: 1.2 meters (later 1.6 meters)
speed: 4–8 knots (depending on engine)

Former commercial rice barges. Capable of carrying a whole rifle company for short distances on calm water. Clumsy. In 1945–1946, *Dévastation* mounted two single twenty-five-millimeter automatic guns aft, three machine guns (two heavy and one light) forward. As finally armed, they mounted one seventy-five-millimeter gun, three mortars, four small automatic guns, and machine guns. Some armor. Often used the more agile LCAs as escorts/scouts.

5. **Landing Craft, Infantry (LCI)**
dimensions/displacement: 160 feet × 24 feet/400 tons
draft: 1.6 meters (laden)
speed: 12 knots (diesels)

Larger craft capable of carrying up to sixty troops in bunks, or two hundred men for short distances on calm water. One seventy-five millimeter gun, two mortars, one forty-millimeter and two twenty-millimeter automatic guns, and machine guns.

6. **Landing Craft, Tank (LCT)**
dimensions/displacement: 120 feet 4 inches × 32 feet/430 tons
draft: 4 feet (laden)
speed: 7 knots (3 diesels)

Larger U.S.-designed craft capable of carrying three to five tanks. Access either end. Built in three sections, bolted together. Two automatic small caliber guns. Some armor. Used on supply and support tasks.

7. **Japanese Barges (war booty)**
   dimensions: 46 feet (steel), 49 feet (wood), 56 feet (steel)
   draft: 3 feet
   speed: 8 knots
       Capable of carrying seventy men or ten tons of cargo. One twin twenty-five-millimeter gun or equivalent. Some side armor.

Appendix D

CHRONOLOGICAL LIST OF FRENCH RETURN TO KEY INDO-CHINESE CITIES AND TOWNS

Saigon	September 12, 1945
Phnom-Penh	October 10
Pakse	October 11
Nha-Trang	October 17
My-Tho	October 25
Vinh-Long	October 29
Can-Tho	October 30
Xuan-Loc	November 3
Tay-Ninh	November 8
Dalat	January 28, 1946
Haiphong	March 8
Savannakhet	March 17
Hanoi	March 18
Tourane	March 26
Hué	March 27
Vientiane	April 25
Dienbienphu	April 26
Luang-Prabang	May 13

Appendix E

GLOSSARY AND ACRONYMS

Aéronavale	French naval air arm
agitprop	propaganda to create action
anciens	old hands
Annamese	people of the three Kys
Bentré (operation)	code name for the return north
"Blanche-Neige"	Snow White (Captain Commentry)
BMEO	Far East Naval (*Fusilier Marin*) Brigade
Bren	British light machine gun
CCS	Anglo-American Combined Chiefs of Staff
CEEO	Far East Expeditionary Corps
C-in-C	commander-in-chief
COMAR	commander naval forces (NOIC)
DGER	French intelligence
DIC	colonial infantry division
dinassaut	combined naval infantry/landing craft unit
"flag"	flagship
FNEO	Far East Naval Forces
Fusilier Marin	naval infantryman

Genesuper	commanding general (theater)
"gun boss"	gunnery officer
"have the con"	exercise control
IJN	Imperial Japanese Navy
JCS	U.S. Joint Chiefs of Staff
Kempetai	Japan's secret police
Ky	Annamese state
landing party	temporary unit drawn from a ship's company to fight ashore
LCA	landing craft, assault
LCI	landing craft, infantry
LCM	landing craft, mechanized
LST	landing ship, tank
Maquis	underground forces
Marine Nationale	French Navy (*La Royale*)
Milice	Vichy militia
nha-qué	average Annamese
NOIC	naval officer in charge
OSS	U.S. Office of Strategic Services
point d'appui	secondary base, naval station
POW	prisoner of war
ratissage	security sweep
RIC	colonial infantry regiment
RN	(British) Royal Navy
Sten	British machine carbine
USN	U.S. Navy
Vichy	the capital of armistice France and, by extension, its government
Viet-Minh	communist-led Annamese political party
"Vieux Charles"	Old Charles (Captain Commentry)
Z (force)	Operation Bentré's naval element

Appendix F

SS *KONTUM*

Kontum (Cie. Cotière d'Annam) was an ancient, single tall-funneled, smoke-belching, steam cargo tramper working the Indochina coast. Measuring at 1,565 tons, she was built in Flensburg (Germany) in 1923. She was scuttled March 10, 1945, in the Mekong Delta, along with most of France's other Far Eastern maritime assets. She was salvaged by the Japanese but escaped to Ceylon, where she was taken into naval service.

Kontum was a member of the first French convoy into Saigon. Prior to Bentré, she delivered a cargo of rice to Haiphong to test the waters. On April 1, 1946, off Cape Saint-Jacques, she struck a mine and sank. She was a long way from Flensburg.

SELECTED BIBLIOGRAPHY

As a rule, only the most authoritative/most recent/most easily available sources have been referenced in the chapter end notes. As should be evident, many more books have been used to put together this story. These sometimes give a better feel for times and places and personalities mentioned. They provide details not otherwise to be found—the memoires are good for this, helpful but not otherwise necessary to the basic story. These have all been included here, for those who might wish to pursue the subject beyond my book. Unfortunately, almost all of the others are in French.

Auphan, Paul, and Jacques Mordal. *La Marine Française dans la Seconde Guerre Mondiale.* Paris: Editions France-Empire, 1976. A standard general work, much revised and updated. There are subtle differences between the French- and English-language versions.

Bernier, Jean-Pierre. *Le Commando des Tigres.* Jacques Grancher, ed. Paris: Maulde et Renou, 1995. The SASB (Commandant Ponchardier) in Indochina, 1945–1946.

Bertrand, Michel. *La Marine Française 1939–40.* La Tour-du-Pin: Editions du Portail, 1984. Encyclopedic reference on the navy, the remains of which showed up here.

Charbonneau, René, and José Maigre. *Les Parias de la victoire: Indochine,*

1945. Paris: Editions France-Empire, 1980. France's position at the close of World War II.
Darrieus, Henri, and Jean Quéguiner. *Historique de la Marine Française (Novembre 1942–Août 1945)*. Saint-Malo: Editions l'Ancre de Marine, 1994. A reference summary, thorough, full of useful data but marred by typos.
Debat, Georges. *Marine Oblige*. Paris: Flammarion, 1974. For the section on life and duty in Saigon, in the early days.
Decoux, Jean. *A la barre de l'Indochine*. Paris: Plon, 1949. Indochina during the Second World War, by the Governor General himself.
Denis, Peter. *Troubled Days of Peace: Mountbatten and South East Asia Command, 1945–46*. Manchester: Manchester University Press, 1987. Saigon was his second priority, only after Singapore.
Favin-Lévêque, Bernard. *Souvenirs de Mer et d'Ailleurs*. Versailles: Editions des 7 Vents, 1990. For the part on duty in the expedition, by a junior officer who held a wide range of assignments and whose friends had more.
de Folin, Jacques. *Indochina 1940–55*. Paris: Perrin, 1993. The end of a dream, by a qualified observer on-scene. Authoritative, unbiased.
Gabrié, Jean. *Les Marines de la Guerre 1935–1945*. Vincennes: Service Historique de la Marine, 1994. A good short summary by another who was there.
Guiberteau, Yannick. *La Dévastation*. Paris: Albin Michel, 1984. One of the Gressier barges as a "river battleship," in Cochin-China. By her captain.
Hooper, Edwin Bickford, Dean C. Allard, and Oscar P. Fitzgerald. *The United States Navy and the Vietnam Conflict: The Setting of the Stage to 1959*. Washington, D.C.: Naval History Division, 1976. Based largely on attaché and other official reports. Good where there was U.S. involvment.
Johnson, Ellis A., and David A. Katcher. *Mines against Japan*. Washington D.C.: Naval Ordnance Laboratory, 1973. Unique, encyclopedic, detailed. Authoritative, by two who helped carry out the program.
Kilian, Robert. *History and Memories: The Naval Infantrymen in Indochina*. Paris: Editions Berger-Levrault, 1948. BNEO by its commanding officer.
King, Ernest J. *U.S. Navy at War 1941–1945*. Washington D.C.: Navy Department, 1946. By the Chief of Naval Operations himself. Assembled from his annual reports.

Koburger, Charles W., Jr. *The Cyrano Fleet: France and Its Navy 1940–1942.* New York: Praeger, 1989. A basic preliminary to this book. Published also in French.

———. *Franco-American Naval Relations 1940–1945.* Westport, Conn.: Praeger, 1994. Concentrates on North Africa, the Mediterranean, and Southern France. Background.

———. *The French Navy in Indochina 1945–54.* New York: Praeger, 1991. Broad, covering ten years, whereas this new book is narrow, covering two years. This new book forms a more detailed preface to the other, in fact.

Ladd, J. D. *Assault from the Sea 1939–45.* London: David and Charles, 1976. British-oriented descriptions of landing ships and craft. Theirs can be quite different from ours.

Marr, David G. *Vietnam 1945: The Quest for Power.* Berkeley: University of California Press, 1995. Extensively documented, using Vietnamese and Japanese as well as Western sources. Tends to follow the Viet-Minh line.

Mauclère, Jean. *Sailors on the Canals.* Paris: J. Peyronnet, 1950. The *Fusiliers Marins* in the early days.

Michel, Jacques, ed. *La Marine Française en Indochine de 1939 à 1955.* Vincennes: Service Historique de la Marine, 1973. Six vols; volume II (Août 1945–Decembre 1946) pertains. An exhaustive, authoritative reference. Includes documents and key reports.

Mordal, Jacques. *The Navy in Indochina.* Paris: Amiot-Dumont, 1953. A readable, early work by a noted naval writer.

Owens, William A. *High Seas: The Naval Passage to an Uncharted World.* Annapolis, Md.: Naval Institute Press, 1995. Emphasizes the coming role of expeditionary warfare. By the vice chairman of the Joint Chiefs of Staff.

Romé, Paul. *Les Oubliés du Bout du Monde.* Paris: Editions Maritimes & d'Outre-Mer, 1983. The war years and the return of the French, by one of the "anciens," a junior officer at the time. He found the Gressier barges.

Sainteny, Jean. *Histoire d'une paix manquée: Indochine, 1945–1947.* Paris: Fayard, 1953. The story, by one of the key players.

Sheehan, Neil, and E. W. Kenworthy. *The Pentagon Papers.* New York: Quadrangle Books, 1971. Monstrous misinterpretation, reflecting Viet-Minh propaganda.

Thierry d'Argenlieu, Georges. *Chronique d'Indochine 1945–1947.* Paris:

Editions Albin Michel, 1985. The political side of the expedition, by the High Commissioner himself.

Trinquier, Roger. *Modern Warfare*. New York: Praeger, 1964. Guerrilla warfare analyzed, in Indochina and Algeria, by a French intelligence colonel.

U.S. Department of Defense. *United States-Vietnam Relations: 1945–1967*. Washington, D.C.: GPO, 1971. The "Pentagon Papers" exhibit inadequate research on Saigon's September 1945 troubles.

Villar, Roger. *Piracy Today*. London: Conway Maritime Press, 1985. Robbery and violence at sea since 1980. By a sometime editor of *Jane's*.

Wassilieff, Alex. *Le Pacha*. Paris: Bernard Grasset, 1980. Fictionalized biography, for the period when he served in Indochina as COMAR Cape Saint-Jacques.

INDEX

l'Aéronavale (naval air arm), 26, 51, 63, 107–8
AFN 1 (Anglo-French support agreement), 28
AFN 2 (Anglo-French support agreement), 29, 51
Aichi Flying Boat, 51, 84
Alessandri (general), 16
Algérien (destroyer), 26, 74, 83, 96, 99
Allied Control Commission, 44, 45, 64
Allied General Order No. 1, 17
Along Bay, 16, 42, 70, 73–74, 101–2
Amphibious capability, 27–28
Amphibious Force, 111
Annam, 62
Annamite (sloop), 26, 51, 53, 55, 83
Arcachonnaise (motorized junk), 57
d'Argenlieu, Georges Thierry (vice admiral/high commissioner): Gaullist, 24, 29, 64, 73, 77, 84, 102, 103, 105–6, 107, 108; resignation, 113
Army-Navy cooperation, 60, 79

Auboyneau, Philippe (vice admiral/COMAR Far East), 25, 63; Commander Force Z, 83, 96–97, 100, 101, 110
Audacieuse (armed junk), 74
"August Uprising," 32–33

Bach-Mai (airstrip), 92
Ban-Me-Thuot, 65
Barfleur (transport), 83, 96, 99, 101
Béarn (aircraft transport), 37, 40, 51, 57, 83, 84, 96, 102
Bentré (Operation), 78–79; modifications, 97; outcome, 102–3; task and plan, 81–82
Bételgeuse (merchantman), 83, 96
Bir-Hacheim (Operation), 91–92
Blanchard (lieutenant), 43, 74
Bogan, Gerald F. (rear admiral/task force commander), 14
Bramaud du Boucheron, François (lieutenant commander), 44, 79

Brazzaville Declaration, 23
British landing craft, 55, 62, 79
Buc-Hoa, 60
Bureau Marine, 79

C-47 (Dakota cargo plane/transport), 84
Camille-Porcher (merchantman), 83
Campha, 74, 108
Camranh Bay, 14, 15, 59, 65; Bentré, 82, 83; Tagne Island, 66
Can-Tho, 56, 57, 61
Cape Saint-Jacques, 41, 49, 51, 65; Bentré, 83
Catalina PBY, 26, 51, 84
Cat-Bi (airfield), 89, 107
Cat-Lai (airfield), 60
Cedile, Jean (colonel/administrator of colonies/commissioner), 45–46
Céphée (merchantman), 83, 96
Cercle Sportif, 67
Chevreuil (sloop), 26, 83, 84, 109
Chang Kai-shek, 32, 70–72, 75–76. See also China
China, 14, 16, 17, 32, 36, 39, 43, 69; accords with French, 75–76, 78, 81, 98; principal player in north, 70–72
Chunking Accords, 75–76, 98
Coastal artillery, 87, 100
Cochin-China, 41, 77–78, 108, 109–10
COMAR Far East, 25, 110
COMAR Haiphong, 84
COMAR Indochina, 63
COMAR Tonkin, 43, 84, 102
Combined Chiefs of Staff (CCS), 18, 27, 78
Commando Ponchardier, 49, 53, 55–56, 61, 83, 92
Commentry, Andre (captain), 43, 44–45, 50–51, 63, 73–74, 79, 102–3
Crayssac (armed launch), 43, 74

Debès (colonel), 109
Decoux, Jean (vice admiral/governor general), 12–14, 16, 29
Devastation (motorized barge), 57
Dinassaut (integrated *Fusilier*-landing craft unit), 58, 60, 103, 111
Dong-Minh-Hoi (political party), 72
Doson, 85, 87, 88, 90
Doudou (landing craft), 57
Doumer Bridge, 92
Dumont-d'Urville (sloop), 109
Duquesne (heavy cruiser), 26, 63, 83

11th Colonial Infantry Regiment (RIC), 47
Emile-Bertin (light cruiser), 26; Force Z role, 83, 96, 100, 102, 105; landing party, 59–60, 63, 65
Eridan (merchantman), 83
Espérance (merchantman), 83

Fai-Tsi-Long Islands, 16, 42, 43, 74. See also Port-Wallut
Fantasque (destroyer-leader), 26, 51, 62, 83, 101, 102
Far East Expeditionary Corps (CEEO): dissolved, 110–11; no defeat, no victory, 113; organization, 24–25, 35–36, 37–38, 38–39, 45, 105
Far East Naval Brigade (BMEO): abolished, 111; expanded, 56–57; organized, 18, 26, 38, 53, 54–56; reorganized, 58–59, 74, 82, 106
Far East Naval Forces (FNEO): organization and mission, 23, 24, 25–28, 49–50, 51, 52, 63–64, 109; reorganized and continued, 110–11
Favin-Lévêque, Bernard (lieutenant), 99–100
Fenard, Raymond (vice admiral), 18

INDEX

5th Colonial Infantry Regiment (RIC), 45, 49–50
Forze Z: concept of maneuver, 89–90; convoy groups, 91; dissolved, 102; mission, 89; off Haiphong, 95, 96; task groups, 96
Foudre (motorized barge), 57
France, 14, 17–18, 22, 29, 34–35, 35–36; Chunking Accords, 75–76; Saigon-Hanoi Accords, 77–78, 105–6, 107; schism, 36–37, 39–40, 43–44
Free French, 13, 36–37, 42, 43–44
French Union, 23, 34, 77–78
Frézouls (armed launch), 43, 74
Fusiliers Marins (naval infantry), 18, 26, 28, 55–56; armored regiment, 81, 113; *dinassauts*, 58, 60, 61

de Gaulle, Charles (brigadier general/provisional president), 12, 22–23, 29
Gaur (Operation), 65–66
Gazelle (sloop), 26, 51, 53, 55, 59, 83, 101
Gia-Lam (airfield), 92
Giap, Vo-Nguyen. See Viet-Minh
Gloire (heavy cruiser), 26, 37, 51, 53; landing party, 59
Gocong, 59, 61
Gracey, Douglas (major general), 44–45, 46–48, 53, 64
Gracieuse (sloop), 66
"Grand Corps." See *Marine Nationale*
la Grandière (colonial gunboat/sloop), 83
Graziani, Gaston (rear admiral), 25, 63
Great Britain, 13, 16–17, 28, 29, 38, 39, 51, 75, 78. See also Mountbatten, Louis; Gracey, Douglas; British landing craft
Gressier barges, 54–55, 56, 58
Guillebon (colonel), 79

Haiphong, 15, 36, 38, 39, 70, 74, 82, 84, 85–87, 87–88, 90, 97, 107–8, 108–9
Hanoi, 12, 32–33, 36, 38, 39, 43, 70, 73, 81, 84, 85, 108, 109–10
Ho Chi Minh (president), 72, 77, 102, 105–6, 107, 108, 110. See also Viet-Minh
Hongay, 59, 74, 81, 84, 85, 87, 90, 97, 108, 109

Imperial Japanese Navy (IJN), 15, 38, 64–65, 88
Indochina, 22–23, 42, 107–8
Indo-Chinese Federation, 23, 77–78, 105
Indo-Chinese *Tirailleurs*, 57

Japan/Japanese, 11–12, 13–15, 19, 21–22, 33, 45, 56, 64–65, 66, 75, 85, 88
Jaubert, François (commander), 54, 56
Jubelin (commander), 62. See also *Triomphant*
Junkers Ju-52 (transport), 84

Kempetai, 15
Khan-Hoa, 65
Kilian, Robert (captain), 54, 56
Kinkaid, Thomas C. (vice admiral, fleet commander), 75, 78
Kontum (merchantman, naval auxiliary), 49, 79–80, 84, 103

Lamotte-Picquet (light cruiser), 14, 43
Landing parties, 59 60
Lave (motorized barge), 57
Leclerc, Jacques (lieutenant general, genesuper): commander Bentré, 79, 91–92, 96–97, 98, 101, 102, 108, 109, 110; commander CEEO,

24–25, 28, 51–52, 53, 64, 73
Lecomte (colonel), 79
Loire 130 (flying boat), 51
Lorientaise (motorized junk), 57
Lu-Han (general), 72, 75–76, 84, 85, 98, 101, 102, 103

MacArthur, Douglas (general of the Army), 24–25, 28, 35
Marine Indochine, 15, 25–28, 44–45, 52, 63, 111
Marine Nationale, 18–19, 23; capabilities, 26–28; schism, 36–37, 38, 39–40, 52, 103, 106
Marinière (landing craft), 57
Merveilleux du Vignaux (captain), 28
Meynier, Robert (commander), 15
Mines, 38, 45, 49, 51, 87–88, 97–98, 99
Minh, Ho-Chi. *See* Ho-Chi-Minh
Mountbatten, Louis (admiral, C-in-C), 13, 16, 17, 21, 28, 29, 39, 44, 64
My-Tho, 15, 55, 57, 61

Nam-Bo, 32, 37, 44, 45, 77
Nam-Dinh, 112–13
Naval Division Far East, 110–11
Naval Forces Far East. *See* Far East Naval Forces (FNEO)
Naval Forces Indochina. *See Marine Indochine*
Naval Infantry River Flotilla, 55–56
Netherlands, 16
Nha-Be, 60
Nha-Trang, 62–63
Nimitz, Chester (admiral of the fleet, C-in-C), 16
9th Colonial Infantry Division (DIC), 81, 82

OSS (Office of Strategic Services), 32, 75

Paimpolaise (Motorized junk), 57
Paris. *See* France
Pentagon Papers, 48
Pétain, Henri (Marshal, chief of state), 22
Philippines, 11–12, 16, 75
Phnom-Penh, 59
Phu-My, 59, 67
Phu-Quoc Islands, 66
Picheral (lieutenant commander), 47
Piracy, 74
Point Edouard, 95, 97, 99, 100
Port-Wallut, 42, 59, 74
Poulo-Condore (island), 66
Princess Beatrix (assault transport), 49

Quang-Yen, 85
Queen Emma (assault transport), 49
Quercy (transport), 38, 51
Quinhon, 90

Rach-Cat, 60
Ramatou (landing craft), 57
Repiton-Préneuf (colonel), 79
Republic of Cochin-China, 108
Republic of Vietnam, 77, 105
Richelieu (fast battleship), 18, 22, 26, 28, 29, 35, 36, 40, 49–50, 53; landing party, 59, 62, 63
de Riencourt (commander), 42, 45
Rivier (lieutenant colonel), 45
Romé, Paul (lieutenant), 54
Roosevelt, Franklin D. (president), 12, 17–18, 39
"La Royale." *See Marine Nationale*

Saigon, 12, 14, 15, 32, 36, 37, 38, 39, 41, 42, 44–45, 45–46; battle for, 46–48, 64, 65, 66–67; Bentré, 82, 83, 84

INDEX   149

Saigon-Hanoi Accords, 77–78, 105
Sainteny, Jean (commandant [major]/
   commissioner), 16, 72–73, 77–78
Saint-Loubert-Bie (merchantman), 83
Salan (general), 78
Sampanière (landing craft), 57
Savorgnan-de-Brazza (colonial gunboat/
   sloop), 26, 83, 101, 109
Scott-Bell (captain), 44, 49, 50–51
Second Armored Division (2nd DB),
   24, 81, 82
Sénégalais (destroyer), 26, 51, 65, 74
Seventh Fleet, 75, 88
6th Colonial Infantry Regiment
   (RIC), 62
Somali (destroyer), 26, 51, 65, 74, 83
Spitfire (fighter-bomber), 84
Suffren (heavy cruiser), 26, 37–38, 51,
   53; landing party, 59, 63–64

Tan-Son-Nhut (airfield), 41, 51
Terror, 33–34, 37, 46, 47–48, 60–61,
   67–68, 107–8, 109–10
Thailand (Siam), 111–12
Thu-Dau-Mot, 65
Tonkin, 13, 16, 69–70
Tonnante (motorized barge), 57
Tourane (Da-Nang), 14
Tourville (heavy cruiser), 26, 63, 65,
   83

Triomphant (destroyer-leader), 18, 22,
   26, 29, 49, 62; at Haiphong, 83,
   96, 98, 99–102
Truman, Harry S. (president), 12, 39
Tu-Ve (Viet militia), 108
23rd Colonial Infantry Regiment
   (RIC), 59

United States, 11–12, 13, 14, 16–17,
   17–18, 19; OSS, 32, 38; policy, 39–
   40, 48, 74–75, 75–76, 87–88, 97–
   98

Vahine (landing craft), 57
Valluy (general), 82, 96, 100, 108
Vichy. See France
Viet-Minh, 31–32, 33–34, 44, 45, 47–
   48, 69, 72, 73; accord with French,
   77–78, 102, 105, 107–8, 109–10;
   no victory, no defeat, 113
Vietnamese Democratic Republic, 72
Vieux-Charles (armed junk), 74
Ville-de-Strasbourg (transport), 38, 51
Vinh-Long, 55–56, 57
VNQDD (the "Dai-Viet" party), 72,
   107
Vu-Yen Cut, 85, 86, 90, 97, 98–99

About the Author

CHARLES W. KOBURGER JR. retired from the U.S. Coast Guard as a reservist with the rank of captain after twenty years of active duty and is now a consultant on maritime affairs. He has published widely on naval and maritime subjects, including *Sea Power in the Twenty-First Century: Projecting a Naval Revolution* (1997), *Pacific Turning Point: The Solomons Campaign, 1942–1943* (1995), *Naval Warfare in the Baltic, 1939–1945: War in a Narrow Sea* (1994), *Franco-American Naval Relations, 1940–1945* (1993), *Naval Warfare in the Eastern Mediterranean: 1940–1945* (1993), and *The French Navy in Indochina: Riverine and Coastal Forces, 1945–1954* (1991), all from Praeger.

CPSIA information can be obtained
at www.ICGtesting.com
Printed in the USA
BVOW06*1752060817
491305BV00003B/5/P